The Gospel of Mark

THE JESUS WE'RE ACHING FOR

LISA HARPER

Lifeway Press® Brentwood, Tennessee

Published by Lifeway Press®

© 2016 Lisa Harper
Reprinted March 2023

Lisa Harper is represented by Alive Literary Agency, 7680 Goddard Street, Suite 200, Colorado Springs, CO, 80920. *www.aliveliterary.com.*

ISBN 978-1-4300-4025-5

Item 005727073

Dewey decimal classification: 226.3

Subject headings: BIBLE. N.T. MARK \ JESUS CHRIST \ GOSPEL

To order additional copies of this resource, write Lifeway Resources Customer Service; 200 Powell Place, Suite 100; Brentwood, TN 37027-7707; Fax order to 615.251.5933; call toll-free 800.458.2772; email orderentry@lifeway.com; or order online at www.lifeway.com.

Printed in the United States of America

Cover design The Visual Rep

Adult Ministry Publishing
Lifeway Resources
200 Powell Place, Suite 100
Brentwood, TN 37027-7707

CONTENTS

ABOUT LISA

Rarely are the terms "hilarious storyteller" and "theological scholar" used in the same sentence, much less used to describe the same person, but Lisa Harper is anything but stereotypical. She is a master storyteller, whose writing and speaking overflows with colorful pop culture references that connect the dots between the Bible and modern life.

Her vocational resume includes six years as the director of Focus on the Family's national women's ministry, followed by six years as the women's ministry director at a large church. Her academic resume includes a master's in theological studies with honors from Covenant Seminary. Now a sought-after Bible teacher and speaker, Lisa is featured on the national Women of Faith tour and speaks at many other large multi-denominational events—such as Christine Caine's *Propel*, Lifeway women's events, and Women of Joy conferences—as well as at hundreds of churches all over the world. She's been on numerous syndicated radio and television programs and was featured on the cover of *Today's Christian Woman*.

Lisa has written 11 books, including *Believing Jesus*, *Stumbling into Grace*, and *A Perfect Mess*. In spite of her credentials, the most noticeable thing about Lisa Harper is her authenticity. "I'm so grateful for the opportunities God's given me," Lisa says, "but don't forget: He often uses donkeys and rocks!"

INTRODUCTION

Since Missy's been home from Haiti for almost two years and is a whopping six years old, I recently added some simple chores to her daily routine so as to help her develop character, a sense of responsibility, and sow some work ethic seeds. For instance, now when we come home from a Target™ run (you know the ones when you planned on just picking up laundry detergent yet somehow walk out with a cart full of gardening paraphernalia and some "deeply discounted" appliance, hair-care product, or quesadilla maker?), she's expected to help me carry in the loot instead of just merrily skipping in front of me empty handed. Unfortunately, her first assistance attempt was a comical train-wreck because when I was looking the other way she dutifully mimicked me and looped one too many plastic bags up her little forearms then toppled over when she attempted to walk toward the house. I'll never forget her darling exasperated expression or the way she protested, "Mama, 'dis is too HAWD!"

This is surely the internal reaction some women have when it comes to Bible study. 'Dis is too hawd! Especially the it's-been-a-while-since-I've-been-in-church or the I've-never-been-in-a-small-group-and-didn't-know-crop-pants-were-required crowd. Because let's admit it—if you've never been in a Bible study before it does appear to be a bit difficult at first what with all the looking up of verses, filling in blanks, and divulging deep thoughts. So let's make a pact that our study of Mark is going to be a safe place to engage with God, OK? That we're going to be the kind of community where every woman feels comfortable asking questions about Him, sharing the highs and lows of her story, and ultimately leans more fully into the arms of the Jesus we're all aching for.

In light of that goal it's not necessary to choose a single group leader for this study (I can almost hear the audible gasps from the type As reading this!), and may actually be more beneficial to choose a couple of friendly chicks to co-lead, because that will help make the environment less personality-driven and more participation-driven.

HERE'S A FEW TIPS TO PROMOTE HEALTHY INVOLVEMENT:

- Establish a no-monopoly chat zone. Encourage everyone to answer at least one question rather than having one big-talker answer all of them.

- Allow for "silence cushions" between questions to give introverts time to for-mulate their thoughts and participate.

- Throw spitballs at anyone who responds to a question with a basic yes-or-no answer. OK, maybe spitballs are a tad punitive, but encourage real responses!

- Be quick to listen and slow to give advice or attempt to fix the other chicks' problems in your circle. Just say no to Dr. Phil wannabes!

- Make your best effort to begin and end on time.

- Don't focus on moving through all the material each time you get together; instead, focus on how your small-group tribe is moving toward Jesus.

In an effort to make Mark user-friendly, we've created a Bible study book geared toward participation instead of intimidation. We've also segmented it into chunks instead of days, so you can complete the questions when you have time—when your baby's sleeping, when your husband's glued to a football game, or when you're finally home from work and have changed into a pair of comfy sweatpants. The last thing we want is to make the homework so cumbersome and time-consuming that your group dwindles down to nonexistent.

Each week starts with a two-page video and group guide. For the first session, you'll just watch the video and get to know each other. Then, during the following week, complete your first week's study. When you gather for the second session, discuss the week 1 study and watch the second session video.

Your format can depend on your group's size. If your group has few members, discuss the previous week's study first and then watch the video, allowing for some time to discuss the video's questions afterward. If you have a large group, you'll probably want to watch the video first and then combine the discussion of video questions and the previous week's work.

Now, may I encourage you to breathe deeply, smile genuinely (even if it's just to yourself), and turn the page? Then doodle wildly in the margins. Be as honest as possible in every response. And fire away with your thoughts, since few questions have right or wrong answers. Feel free to throw this Bible study book on the floor with gusto if something I've written steps on one of your emotional bruises—or hug it close to your chest when Jesus whispers how valuable you are to Him while you're perusing a passage.

My sincere hope and fervent prayer is that the King of all kings will woo us closer to Himself than ever before this season. That Holy Spirit—our Comforter and Counselor—will seal in us a profound assurance of God's compassion. And that greater comprehension of His love for us will lead to us becoming more passionate ambassadors of His gospel. I simply Can. Not. Wait. to see how our Savior shows up as we run hard toward Him together! In the meantime, please know that I'm honored and delighted to get to take this divine journey with you.

Warmest regards,

SESSION 1. HOLD ME, PLEASE

Biblical scholars agree that the Book of Mark was the _____ _____ written.

The word gospel, euangelion *in Greek, means _____ _____.*

Not only is Mark the first Gospel, predating Matthew, Luke, and John, but it is based on the apostolic _____ of _____.

The Book of Acts records the gathering of the first _____ _____.

Despite the early losses in their lives, Peter and John Mark went on to be remembered not as _____ but as _____.

Two Reasons for the Urgency Expressed in the Book of Mark

1. Peter and John Mark _____ the undeserved compassion of Jesus.

2. The compassion their first century _____ was so desperate for.

During the first century, the world was under the dominion of _____.

Our ache accelerates Jesus' _____. And the heart of God is _____ by the wounds of mankind.

Video sessions available for purchase at
www.lifeway.com/GospelofMark

Discussion Questions:

What drew you to study the Gospel of Mark and what are some facts you already knew about Mark—the man or the Gospel?

What is one thing from the video teaching that was new to you or you found interesting?

What do you hope to gain most from this Bible study? Discuss a few goals you hope to accomplish through this study.

AGGRESSIVE GRACE

REAL LIFE

"The hardness of God is kinder than the softness of men."[1]

C.S. LEWIS

I wasn't what you'd describe as an actively disobedient kid. I mean if my parents specifically told me not to do something, I typically complied. For instance, when mom brought my baby brother, John Price, home from the hospital she gave me a lengthy excursus about the soft spot on the top of his head before allowing me to hold him.

I'd anxiously anticipated playing with John Price for months and months, but I heeded mom's sober warning about how if I accidentally poked a sharp object like a fork, a screwdriver, or even my pointer finger into that tender spot where his tiny skull hadn't completely closed yet I could cause him irreparable brain damage. I decided to stick to my normal extracurricular routine of climbing trees, playing freeze tag with the Brooks kids, and riding my bike in the glorious wake of fog that trailed the mosquito truck on warm summer evenings instead.

It doesn't take a genius to figure out that cruising a purple Schwinn with glittering streamers and a banana seat through a cloud of carcinogens is way better than accidentally poking a hole in some floppy baby's head and causing his guts to squirt out all over everything. Gross, who needs that kind of drama? Not only did I heed mom's warning when it came to J.P.'s fragile fontanel, I carefully inscribed a huge "X" on the top of his head with a black indelible marker when mom wasn't looking just in case some clueless stranger got close to my little brother's noggin with a mechanical pencil or one of those things bearded Vermont men stab into trees to get maple syrup. Family lore has it that it took months for the big, black "X" to fade, thereby prompting questions from passersby if mom forgot to put on his baby beanie before taking him out in public!

One can never be too careful about accidentally causing a sibling's head to erupt.

Matthew, Mark, and Luke are formally classified as the Synoptic Gospels, which means they are similar in their content and literary style (synoptic: 1. pertaining to or constituting a synopsis; affording or taking a general view of the principal parts of a subject. 2. taking a common view; used chiefly in reference to the first three Gospels, Matthew, Mark and Luke, from their similarity in content, order, and statement).[2] The literary style and content of John's Gospel account differs significantly from the first three (i.e. he doesn't include parables yet does include unique Christological experiences like the washing of the disciple's feet), which is why his recording of Jesus' earthly life and ministry is not classified as synoptic.

However, if my parents neglected to forbid me to do something, well then it was fair game. Like when they neglected to tell me that it wasn't a good idea to leave a nice girl's eighth grade slumber party in the middle of the night with a wild girl who thought she knew a shortcut to the McDonald's that was twelve miles away by car. At the time it sounded logical—even compassionate—to traipse across town at two in the morning to bring back nourishment for our peers. Good night, if those survival reality television shows were popular in the late '70s, we probably would've been lauded for our brave ingenuity instead of being firmly reprimanded by two policemen when we came limping back to the soirée around noon, several hours after our empty sleeping bags were discovered.

After enduring the emotive sobs and entreaties of said good girl (who felt very betrayed that we didn't invite her to accompany us on the ill-fated adventure), the frosty disapproval of her parents, and a second, even harsher, reprimand from mom and Dad Angel (my stepfather) on the way home, I decided it would be best not to disclose the nasty cut on the bottom of my right foot that was a result of stepping on a broken bottle while wearing flip flops on the trek.

Would you typically rather suffer in silence after doing something stupid or deal with the negative repercussions immediately and up-front? Why?

When the cut began to throb that night, I held my foot over the bathtub, doused it with rubbing alcohol, wrapped it in an Ace™ bandage, and made a mental note to wear sturdier footwear if I ever went on another nighttime excursion. When it hurt too badly to stand on the next morning, I told mom I thought I was coming down with the flu—a white lie she swallowed whole after taking my temperature and finding it to be unusually high.

Later that day mom asked if I had omitted anything from the slumber-party-disappearance story, so I finally confessed everything. When she lifted the sheet she saw the angry red streaks—signs of a serious infection—running up and down my leg. She bundled me into the Buick and raced to the hospital where a white-headed doctor with protruding Albert-Einstein-ish eyebrows told me, "This is going to hurt something awful, honey, but we don't have time for you to get numb if we're going to save your foot!" I don't remember much else after seeing the flash of his scalpel and watching mom slump into a plastic chair to keep from fainting.

For centuries, Saint Augustine's view that Matthew was written prior to Mark prevailed in theological circles. That is, until the middle of the nineteenth century when a debate called "The Synoptic Problem" arose in academic circles. After careful study of the interrelationships of the four Gospels many scholars eventually agreed it was more likely that Mark was actually the first Gospel account recorded (officially titled "The Markan Hypothesis"). With a few notable exceptions the priority of Mark is now the view widely held by modern theological tradition.[3]

Now I knew from the moment I stepped on that broken bottle that it was a nasty cut, but I assumed it was nothing a little rubbing alcohol couldn't cure. I was more concerned about whether it would keep me from competing in the track meet later that week. Or whether I would get grounded if mom found out about the injury. The concern that weighed most heavily on my adolescent mind was whether I'd lose phone privileges, which would surely render me a 13 year-old pariah. That I could lose my foot or possibly even my life never occurred to me.

What concern weighs most heavily on your mind today?

Describe at least one example when you resembled the old adage "couldn't see the forest for the trees" in your walk of faith.

Read 2 Peter 1:3-11. How would you synopsize this passage into one sentence?

How would you describe the connection Peter made between *perspective* and *perseverance* (pay special attention to verse 9)?

REAL TRUTH

Mark 2 tells how one man's greatest concern pales next to Jesus' far-greater compassion:

> A few days later, when Jesus came back to Capernaum, the news
> spread that he was at home. Many people gathered together so
> that there was no room in the house, not even outside the door.
> And Jesus was teaching them God's message. Four people came,
> carrying a paralyzed man. Since they could not get to Jesus because
> of the crowd, they dug a hole in the roof right above where he was
> speaking. When they got through, they lowered the mat with the
> paralyzed man on it. When Jesus saw the faith of these people, he
> said to the paralyzed man, "Young man, your sins are forgiven."
> MARK 2:1-5, NCV

Notice that neither the paralytic, nor his buddies, asked for forgiveness. They went to great lengths in their quest for physical healing. The man humbled himself to the point of being dead weight. He allowed his homies to lug him across town to a Bible study in a house because he heard the guest rabbi was a healer. But when they neared the address, cars lined the entire street and they couldn't even find a place in the yard.

I wonder what the man thought when he realized he couldn't get close to the Healer. Perhaps he closed his eyes and sighed heavily, thinking, *I knew this was a long shot. Why did I allow myself to get my hopes up again? Maybe it is time for me to let the dream of walking go. Maybe I should stop hoping for more and just make the best of what is.*

We can only speculate what the paralyzed man was thinking. None of his words are recorded, much less his thoughts. Still, Mark specified that his friends' faith moved Jesus, possibly implying his lack thereof. So I can't help wondering if his heart was sinking after being toted all over town to no avail. Did he protest when his cohorts jostled him up the stairs to the roof and cut a hole into the sure-to-be-furious homeowner's ceiling?

If I was the one being lowered and rudely interrupting Jesus' sermon, I think misgivings would've been racing through my mind. Apologies would have poured from my mouth faster than the mud and straw could rain down on the less-than-amused guests.

Wouldn't you love to know what the paralyzed man was thinking in that moment? Was he hopeful that a cure was within reach or humiliated that his need was out in the open for all to see? Maybe he felt some of both.

How do you think you'd respond in that situation if you were the one being lowered?

What about if you were one of the Bible study attendees who was being showered with debris?

Describe a time when one of your private needs was publicly exposed (e.g., when your child got expelled from school for drinking or when someone told you they were praying for your marital and/or financial troubles even though you hadn't shared that particular request with them). How did the unexpected exposure make you feel?

READ JAMES 5:13-18. The beginning of this passage distills the Christian life to a profoundly simple application: If you're hurt, PRAY to God. If things are going well for you, PRAISE Him. In the past year, which exercise of faith have you found yourself practicing more often, prayer or praise? Why?

Regardless of what was racing through the paralytic's mind when his gurney jerked to a halt in front of Jesus, the comfort that flooded him following our Redeemer's response surely eclipsed it:

And when Jesus saw their faith, he said to the paralytic,
"Son, your sins are forgiven."
MARK 2:5

The Greek word *son* here is *teknon* or "child." [4] It's a tender term of acceptance and affection much like the pet name I called Missy this morning. When she asked if she could have orange juice with her breakfast, I said, "Of course, baby." She's my little girl and I love her with all my heart. I would've been willing to walk to the grocery store and fetch her orange juice. Since the day God allowed me to bring her home from Haiti, Missy has never felt like a burden to me. In fact, I actually enjoy meeting her needs—whether it's getting her beverage of choice from the fridge or giving her a twice daily dose of HIV meds—because She's. My. Kid.

THE JEWISH BIBLE is also known as the *Tanakh*. *Tanakh* is not a word but an acronym, T-N-K, based on the three divisions of the Hebrew Bible—Torah (the Law), Nevi'im (the Prophets), and Ketuvim (the Writings). [5]

Whose needs do you typically enjoy meeting?

What sort of needs tend to make you feel burdened or resentful?

Missy doesn't usually ask for the three anti-retroviral medications that are keeping the human immunodeficiency virus at bay in her bloodstream. Since she just turned six, she doesn't yet understand that without those meds the virus—now undetectable in her little body—would begin to replicate and grow. Her currently beefy immune system would be compromised, leaving her vulnerable to infection and disease. Without the meds I carefully measure and supervise her swallowing every morning and every night, her HIV might progress into full-blown AIDS. Furthermore, my Punkin's prescriptions don't taste good (I have yet to understand why they don't make bubblegum or grape flavored meds for kids since there are millions of cases of pediatric HIV but I digress), so taking meds is not the most pleasant part of her day.

So I bought the cutest, kid-oriented pill pouches and syringes I could find. I made up a silly song and dance routine to make med-time more fun. You'd better bet I am conscientiously committed to ensuring my daughter takes the medicine she doesn't have the foresight to ask for yet, because as the reasonable adult in our relationship, I know they're saving her life.

If only I could walk again, everything would be OK, had surely crossed the paralytic's mind more than once. But our Savior knew that desire wasn't remotely big enough. He knew fixing the man's legs wouldn't fix the gaping hole in his heart. Our Creator Redeemer knew that simply becoming ambulatory couldn't restore the soul-crippling affliction of being separated from God. So the Messiah went beyond the paralytic's immediate comprehension of need. The King lavished the paralytic with infinitely more treasure than he had the foresight to ask. Jesus dispensed forgiveness—a prescription paid for with His own blood. He didn't just heal the man's legs; He saved the man's life.

The pardon Jesus handed the paralytic revealed that he wasn't asking audaciously enough—that his greatest desire was still too dinky. Would you describe the prayers you've been praying lately as audacious or anemic? Explain why.

READ MARK 11:22-24. What's the most audacious "mountain tossed into the sea" prayer request on your heart this season? Do you feel like you're whispering it toward heaven with hesitation and trepidation or bellowing it to the Heavenly Father who delights in meeting your needs?

READ MATTHEW 9:10-13 AND MARK 2:15-17. The Pharisees were considered to be very bright scholars—especially in light of their largely illiterate culture—but they were slow on the uptake when it came to recognizing their own spiritual neediness. Describe a situation when it took awhile for it to dawn on you that you were spiritually "sick" as well and desperately needed the healing only Jesus can offer.

REAL ACHE

Decades ago, before God spanked me and gave me multiple time-outs for the sin of gossip and before I realized that most of Nashville's iconic music community is somehow connected or related, I shoved my foot so far into my proverbial mouth it's a wonder it didn't get lodged there forever. I was making small talk with a few people who worked for a record label in town following a concert by a singer/songwriter whose warbling had fallen far short of harmonic. So, wanting to sound like the savvy musical connoisseur I wasn't, I said something along of the lines of, "Her gifts as a lyricist are noticeably stronger than her gifts as a vocalist." Of course, I knew immediately by the raised eyebrows and everyone's sudden obsession with the carpeting that I'd said something that had dramatically changed our group dynamic. We'd shifted from a superficial, albeit friendly, conversation to an awkward, almost hostile silence. It wasn't until many uncomfortable minutes later that a compassionate acquaintance pulled me aside and explained that the artist I'd so rudely maligned was the wife of one of them in the circle!

When Jesus called the paralytic "son" and then pronounced his sins forgiven, it triggered a dramatic shift in that first century Capernaum crowd too:

> When Jesus saw the faith of these people, he said to the paralyzed man, "Young man, your sins are forgiven." Some of the teachers of the law were sitting there, thinking to themselves, "Why does this man say things like that? He is speaking as if he were God. Only God can forgive sins." Jesus knew immediately what these teachers of the law were thinking. So he said to them, "Why are you thinking these things? Which is easier: to tell this paralyzed man, 'Your sins are forgiven,' or to tell him, 'Stand up. Take your mat and walk'? But I will prove to you that the Son of Man has authority on earth to forgive sins." So Jesus said to the paralyzed man, "I tell you, stand up, take your mat, and go home." Immediately the paralyzed man stood up, took his mat, and walked out while everyone was watching him. The people were amazed and praised God. They said, "We have never seen anything like this!"
> MARK 2:5-12, NCV

The more common term for "unclean spirit" (Mark 1:23) is "demon," which is used 63 times in the New Testament. Here's what we know about demons according to Scripture:

• Demonic forces are likely made up of the angels who fell with Satan in his rebellion against God (Rev. 12:4).

• Some demons roam freely (Mark 1:21-34); others are confined (2 Pet. 2:4; Jude 6).

• They are powerful personalities, although not omnipotent (Mark 1:24).

• Their activity may have increased during the time of Christ and will do so again in the coming end times (Rev. 6–19).

• They are set up under Satan's control (Eph. 6:11-12), probably in rank and possibly in geography (Dan. 10:10-13).

• They have limited authority and can promote disunity, propagate false doctrine, inflict disease, cause mental difficulties, and hinder Christian growth.

• Demons can oppress but not possess Christ-followers.[6]

Prior to this incident people had been astonished and impressed by the authority of Jesus. In chapter one, after witnessing Jesus heal a demoniac, the crowd is described as "amazed" (Mark 1:27). But now, for the first time, His miraculous authority made some people mad. The toes He stepped on here were significant, too. He offended the Pharisees, who were reputed to be among the smartest, holiest, and most devout among Jewish men. Yet in spite of the fact that He was well aware He'd rubbed these religious leaders the wrong way, Jesus knew immediately what they were thinking, so He asked them:

"Why do you question this in your hearts?"
MARK 2:8, NLT

He didn't back down. Not even slightly.

Some of the early Christians were so passionate about their faith in Jesus that they were accused of turning the world upside down. Our Christian ancestors ticked off entire towns and got themselves in gobs of hot water (e.g., Acts 17:1-9).

Have you ever offended someone because your faith in Christ was too bold for their liking? If so, what did you specifically do or say that set them off?

READ 2 CORINTHIANS 2:14-16. Describe a situation in which you think it's not only appropriate but even necessary to be "offensive"—or as Paul puts it here, "to those who are perishing, we are a dreadful smell of death and doom" (v.16, NLT)—to unbelievers?

READ PROVERBS 27:6. In the context of being a false flatterer or an honest true friend—even when the truth stings—how would you rate yourself?

1	2	3	4	5	6
Significant Suck-Up			Compassionate Toe Crusher		

In fact, if you'll join me and leapfrog over the passage about Jesus' commissioning a less-than-scrupulous IRS agent (Matthew) to be a disciple and sharing a message that included an interesting wineskin metaphor (Mark 2:13-22), we'll get to two more politically incorrect encounters of Christ where He dances on top of even more dangerous feet:

One Sabbath day, as Jesus was walking through some fields of grain, his followers began to pick some grain to eat. The Pharisees said to Jesus, "Why are your followers doing what is not lawful on the Sabbath day?"

Jesus answered, "Have you never read what David did when he and those with him were hungry and needed food? During the time of Abiathar the high priest, David went into God's house and ate the holy bread, which is lawful only for priests to eat. And David also gave some of the bread to those who were with him."

Then Jesus said to the Pharisees, "The Sabbath day was made to help people; they were not made to be ruled by the Sabbath day. So then, the Son of Man is Lord even of the Sabbath day."

Another time when Jesus went into a synagogue, a man with a crippled hand was there. Some people watched Jesus closely to see if he would heal the man on the Sabbath day so they could accuse him.

Jesus said to the man with the crippled hand, "Stand up here in the middle of everyone."

Then Jesus asked the people, "Which is lawful on the Sabbath day: to do good or to do evil, to save a life or to kill?" But they said nothing to answer him.

Jesus was angry as he looked at the people, and he felt very sad because they were stubborn. Then he said to the man, "Hold out your hand." The man held out his hand and it was healed. Then the Pharisees left and began making plans with the Herodians about a way to kill Jesus.
MARK 2:23–3:6, NCV

Jesus had already caused the Pharisees' eyebrows to twitch when He pronounced the paralytic's sins forgiven, but now He catapulted off the ledge of Jewish propriety by proclaiming the futility of religiosity and Himself preeminent over the Sabbath—a cornerstone of Jewish faith. Yikers, talk about incendiary! The Messiah may as well have waved a giant red cape in front of an itching-to-gore-a-matador bull.

God gave Moses the Law on Mount Sinai (Ex. 20–31). *Torah* (meaning *law*) refers to the first five books of Scripture or to the Law within the books. Later Jewish scholars codified lists of laws—which they also called *torah*. The later Jewish teachers created a system derived from the Law for both communal order and connection with God. You cannot overstate the significance of this Law in orthodox Jewish culture. You could liken it to the scaffolding of their entire people group—it held them up and held them together. Yet while the Law was relatively effective as an infrastructure and system of worship, it never ever had the power to redeem sinners. God didn't give Moses the Law so that by it we could be saved but that by it we could recognize our need for a Savior!

Why do you think following religious rules makes most of us feel more justified or secure in our faith?

What's an example of something you've done mainly just to cause other Christians to think you're spiritually mature?

READ MATTHEW 23. How would you synopsize Jesus' sermon (often referred to as "The Seven Woes") about the futility of religious activity in a book or movie title?

Since picking grain on the Sabbath was one of the thirty-nine types of work or activity the Jewish priesthood had decided was a sin, that's the first molehill the Pharisees tried to turn into a mountain:

As his disciples made a path, they pulled off heads
of grain. The Pharisees told on them to Jesus: "Look,
your disciples are breaking Sabbath rules!"
MARK 2:24, THE MESSAGE

I can only imagine the steam coming out of their haughty ears when Jesus affirmed the basic premise of Sabbath (physical rest) but went on to assert Himself as the Lord of the Sabbath in light of His unique ability to provide the spiritual rest for which humanity is desperate:

Then Jesus said to the Pharisees, "The Sabbath day was made
to help people; they were not made to be ruled by the Sabbath
day. So then, the Son of Man is Lord even of the Sabbath day."
MARK 2:27-28, NCV

Therefore it comes as no surprise that they're depicted as vultures in the next scene—watching Jesus' every move with a predatory glare from the top row of the synagogue bleachers:

Another time Jesus went into the synagogue, and a man with a shriveled
hand was there. *Some of them were looking for a reason to accuse Jesus,
so they watched him closely* to see if he would heal him on the Sabbath.
MARK 3:1-2, NIV (EMPHASIS MINE)

I've been in a fluffy season for more than a decade now—interspersed with brief periods of leanness when I can actually feel my hip bones while lying down on my back—therefore I've been to multiple Weight Watchers® and Jenny Craig® "weigh-ins." And the one thing I've noticed is that no matter what the time of day or time of year, most of us wear as little as possible when we weigh in. It might be the middle of an ice storm in February but doggone it, I'm still going to wear the thinnest nylon running pants or shorts in my closet, a wisp of a T-shirt and flip flops or shoes I can easily slip off. I don't even wear much jewelry on those terrible, horrible, no good, standing-on-the-scale-next-to-a-perky-weight-management-counselor days because Every. Single. Ounce. Counts!

Defining your relationship with God solely based on the Law can be just as depressing because Every. Single. Infraction. Counts. Every impatient word while stuck in traffic. Every unkind thought in a slow checkout line at the grocery store. Every lapse in judgment. Every minute of insecurity. They all add up to tip the scale toward fantastically flawed. No perfectly law-abiding human exists. Paul says it bluntly and succinctly in Romans 3:

For all have sinned, and come short of the glory of God.
ROMANS 3:23, KJV

No wonder the Pharisees were grouchy; they were surely exhausted from trying to uphold the façade of moral perfection! Sadly, instead of owning up to their faults and receiving forgiveness and healing from the One who already knew the truth about them anyway, their hard hearts withered to the point of conspiring with the Herodians to kill Him.

I'll try not to bore you with a long missive on the disparity between the Pharisees and the Herodians, but that they put aside their huge animosity toward each other to form an alliance against Jesus is significant. The Herodians represented the ruling power and hedonistic culture of Rome. They were pluralistic, polytheistic pagans. They acted like entitled fraternity boys with fat wallets and no scruples. Herodians were the absolute opposite of the pursed-lipped, allergic-to-fun, law-abiding Pharisees.

That these crews came together to take down the Son of God is as radical a concept as the leaders of the red states and the blue states coming together to back the same presidential candidate. It highlights the shocking similarity between unrestrained immorality—*I'm going to do whatever feels good to me in the moment!*—and restrained moral conformity—*I'm going to follow the rules better than anyone else even if it kills me!* In both cases, the practitioner is attempting to be their own god. And both approaches lead to self-righteousness. To an ironic "we're so much better than people who think they're better than other people" arrogance. Isn't it interesting how pious pew warmers can actually form a subconscious alliance with irreligious partiers?

> What similar personality traits have you noticed in modern day Pharisees and wild-as-a-buck partiers who avoid Christianity like the plague?

Which extreme—secularism or religious conformity—do you tend to gravitate toward if you're not careful? Why do you think that is your temptation?

Someone once said, "Every saint has a past, and every sinner has a future." Do you think it's important to remember our past failures and if so, why?

When has your disappointment with your past failures driven you further away from the forgiveness and healing of Jesus? When has your disappointment with your past failures driven you to Him?

Last week—when I was in emotional high weeds because I had so much work to do in order to meet the deadline for this study—I was sitting at the kitchen table typing and realized my cell phone wasn't next to my laptop, where I was pretty sure I'd left it. Missy was comfortably sprawled out on the couch about twenty feet away watching *The Fox and The Hound* (one of her favorite Disney classics), so I called out, "Hey honey, have you seen my phone?" To which she chirped happily, "Yes ma'am!" I got up from the table and walked over to her and asked, "Baby, I need to check something on my phone so will you please tell me where it is?" She grinned mischievously and replied, "I put it in a drawah, mama!" I wasn't feeling especially tolerant at the time but realizing she thought we were playing a game, I tried to play along, "OK, baby, how about you show me what drawer you chose to hide mama's phone in?" She bounced to her feet and began skipping from room to room, opening drawer after drawer, none of which contained my phone.

After about fifteen minutes of the increasingly frustrating routine of Missy emphatically declaring, "It's in 'dis drawah, mama!" only to find that it wasn't, and after I'd stopped the festivities several times to clarify how important it was for her to show me where she'd hidden my phone (Missy's only been speaking English for 15 months and sometimes there's still a communication gap), I reached the bottom of my patient parent bucket. I knelt down to her level, looked directly into her beautiful brown eyes, and said in a very firm tone that sounded shockingly like the one my mother used with me when I misbehaved at Missy's age, "Melissa, this Is. Not. Funny. At. All. If you don't show me where you put my phone right now I will turn off the movie and you're going to bed early." Of course, her eyes filled with crocodile tears and her bottom lip began to tremble, but since I think consistency is critical in parenting, I followed through by putting my hand on her tiny shoulder and herding her to her bedroom, turning the TV off in route much to her dismay.

A little while later, I came trudging back downstairs with a sagging spirit because I don't enjoy disciplining Missy even though I know it's for her good. Plus, I was fretting about the fact that I didn't have time to go to the Apple store to get a new phone the next day, not to mention dreading what crucial data had been gobbled from my iPhone innards never to be seen again by the ubiquitous, carnivorous "cloud." Sadness, frustration, and worry were getting their party started in my head when I glanced at the Bible next to my laptop and wondered, "What is that weird lump in my study Bible?" Before I flipped it open to find the "missing" phone, my heart had already begun its swift descent to my stomach. It's a wonder the Holy Spirit didn't zap my posterior with lightning as I bolted back upstairs to Missy's room to apologize.

I sat down on the edge of her bed and took her hand in mine, but before I was able to explain why I was sorry, her face split into a grin, she blurted out sincerely, "Dat's okay, mama. I lub you!", wrapped her arms around me, and squeezed. My tenderhearted baby girl is so uncomfortable when she feels distance between us that she jumped the gun and forgave me before I even had time to confess! Which left me as the one with hot tears running down my face (only mine weren't of the dramatic, large lizard variety).

The thing that slays me more than anything else in the passages we've pondered thus far in Mark's Gospel account is the fact that Jesus forgave the paralytic and the dude didn't even repent! In fact, as best I can tell, this is the only encounter in the Gospels when Jesus' redemption wasn't somehow associated with repentance, either professed by the sinner, like when Peter recognized he was a hot mess after Jesus orchestrated a miraculous catch of fish and said, "Depart from me, for I am a sinful man, O Lord" (Luke 5:8b)—or commanded by Christ Himself, like when He lavishly forgave the chick who'd been caught in adultery but added the admonition, "Go, and from now on sin no more" when He sent her on her way (John 8:11b).

So does that mean Mark was attempting to vault over a compulsory doctrinal element or pervert salvific principles? Nope. It means that Jesus was so incredibly eager to restore the paralytic into a right relationship with his Heavenly Father that He preempted the guy's repentance (which Jesus foreknew because He's omnipotent) with mercy. I don't know about you, but the idea of Jesus pursuing me with aggressive grace puts me in the mood to admit my mistakes much faster!

> When have you experienced the grace of God totally apart from your own seeking it?

Bestselling author Anne Lamott wrote, "Grace means you're in a different universe from where you had been stuck, when you had absolutely no way to get there on your own."[7]

What (or who) has God's grace gotten you "unstuck" from recently?

One of my favorite living pastors/authors/theologians is Dr. Tim Keller of Redeemer Presbyterian Church in New York. I listened to his entire sermon series on Mark (titled "King's Cross" and available at *www.gospelinlife.com*) while researching Mark. And one of the remarkable things he said—among many—is this: "Religion teaches, 'I obey, therefore I'm accepted.' The Gospel teaches, 'I'm completely accepted, therefore I obey.'"[8]

In other words, when our hearts have been transformed by the unconditional love of Jesus Christ, the moral law reminds us of what He accomplished on the cross for us and stimulates humility. We set our course toward holiness not in an attempt to justify ourselves but as a grateful response to the One who lovingly rescued us from that awful, accusatory scale!

What end does God accomplish through His kindness according to Romans 2:4?

How has God's mercy steered you toward repentance lately?

READ EXODUS 34:6. Describe a time when you messed up so badly, you were afraid you were going to be on the receiving end of a lightening bolt—or at least something super punitive—and instead experienced the tangible compassion of Christ.

How did you respond to His kindness?

READ MARK 2:18-22. Has the Holy Spirit given you any fresh spiritual insight through the Gospel of Mark yet? If so, what?

THE GOSPEL OF MARK: AN INTRODUCTION

Throughout most of Christian history, many people saw Mark's Gospel as short, incomplete, and impatient—basically a hasty abridgment of the Gospels of Matthew and Luke. Its status as being genuine Scripture was always secure. Yet among the Synoptic Gospels, some New Testament scholars thought Mark to be less important than the fuller accounts of Matthew and Luke. The early church was especially interested in Matthew since common consensus held that it was the oldest Gospel account. This evaluation held for centuries, but views about relations and chronologies for the Synoptics shifted once New Testament theologians began in-depth comparative studies.

In the nineteenth century, many scholars began to indicate they believed Mark had actually preceded Matthew and Luke. Further, they theorized that Matthew and Luke used Mark as a prototype and source when authoring their own accounts. They called this theory the "Markan Priority." Scholars who denied biblical inspiration concluded that Matthew and Luke embellished and expanded Mark's account to create a more robustly divine Jesus. Discerning evangelical scholars, however, rejected such skepticism. They accepted the Markan Priority, affirming that Mark was the earliest of the Synoptics and that Matthew and Luke each used Mark's Gospel as one of their sources. This interpretation did not diminish their understanding that the Holy Spirit indeed inspired the Gospel writers in their work. Further, by seeing Mark as the oldest and foundational for the three Synoptics, these scholars began to investigate how Matthew and Luke handled Mark's material as the Spirit led them. This Mark-as-foundational understanding allowed scholars to discern what special emphases each Gospel writer wished to bring to the forefront for their chosen audiences. The Markan Priority lifted Mark's Gospel from the shadows, giving it a prominence that it retains to this day.

AUTHORSHIP

Like the others, Mark's Gospel is anonymous. The epigram "According to Mark" was added some time after Mark composed his work, possibly by A.D. 125. Long-standing tradition identifies this Mark as John Mark of the New Testament. John Mark's mother hosted meetings of early believers in her Jerusalem home during the early days of Christianity (Acts 12:12). This put Mark within the sphere of apostles and eyewitnesses to Jesus' life. In fact, Mark accompanied Paul on his first missionary journey, but deserted the endeavor at Perga and returned to Jerusalem (13:13). Traveling with Paul would have provided Mark with an excellent chance to learn the content of Paul's preaching about

Adapted from "The Gospel of Mark: An Introduction" by Jeremy R. Howard, *Biblical Illustrator*, Fall 2009, 7-10.

Christ. Mark was later restored to Paul's confidence, giving him additional chances to glean vital biographical data that Paul had gathered about Jesus (2 Tim. 4:11).

Mark also enjoyed the benefit of learning under the personal tutelage of Simon Peter, the stalwart and passionate companion of Jesus during His earthly ministry. So familiar was Peter with Mark that he goes so far as to call him "my son" (1 Pet. 5:13). Arguably Peter had greater influence on Mark than Paul did. Early tradition even held that Mark's Gospel was written as a reflection of Peter's preaching. In approximately, A.D. 325, the church historian Eusebius recorded a portion of Bishop Papias' writings. Speaking of the origins of the Gospel of Mark, Papias said, "Mark being the interpreter of Peter whatsoever he recorded he wrote with great accuracy but not however, in the order in which it was spoken or done by our Lord."[9] The biblical evidence for John Mark's close relationships with Peter and Paul, and the early church unanimously attributing this account to Mark, help to establish him firmly as the author.

DATE AND AUDIENCE

Putting a precise date to Mark's Gospel is not possible. Skeptics assume Mark must have been written sometime after the fall of Jerusalem in A.D. 70 since, in their view, Jesus' supernatural prophecies had to have been added after those events (Mark 13:2).

However, evidence suggests a date in the mid-60s or earlier. For instance, some scholars hold that the Book of Acts ends with events that actually date to around A.D. 62. Luke obviously wrote his Gospel before his Book of Acts—meaning he wrote his Gospel before 62. Further, given the likelihood that Mark was written before Luke, we can reasonably date Mark to A.D. 60 or earlier. This is a well-attested view in current scholarship.[10]

A second possibility is that Mark was written in the middle or late 60s, before the destruction of Jerusalem in A.D. 70. This theory is based on the assumption that Papias was implying that Mark wrote his Gospel after Peter's death. This theory is weakened, though, by the fact that other early opinions (like that of Clement of Alexandria) held that Peter was alive when Mark was written. If Peter were indeed alive, this would mean Mark wrote his Gospel in the 50s.

Evidence—such as Mark's use of Latin terms and general emphasis on suffering, both of which the Christians in Rome could well understand—seems also to indicate Mark wrote while in Rome. Further, early Christian tradition affirmed that Mark was in Rome when he wrote his Gospel.

MARK TODAY

Mark has risen from obscurity in the past century and now has a place of prominence in studies of the Gospels. Likewise it should rank high in the attentions of Jesus' followers today, for in this urgent little Gospel we are admonished to give our all to the Son who has given His all for us.

SESSION 2. THE PRICE OF DISCIPLESHIP AND THE INVALUABLE PRIZE OF A FOREVER FAMILY

Jesus' choosing exactly 12 disciples is likely a New Testament nod to the 12 _____ in the Old Testament.

The Zealots were a _____ group committed to overthrowing _____.

Jesus can mend even the most difficult _____.

Jesus is the only One with infinite _____ who has the capacity to meet the _____ needs of everyone around you.

All of us come to a point of faith in our life where the _____ of discipleship is _____ than we were prepared to pay.

Jesus has to come _____.

When being a Christian gets tough, the way we must persevere is to keep our eyes on the _____ _____.

The end game for us is the invaluable prize of being _____ into Jesus' forever family.

The ache all of us have to belong in a safe, loving, nurturing _____ is perfectly _____ in the person of Jesus Christ.

Video sessions available for purchase at
www.lifeway.com/GospelofMark

Discussion Questions:

Glance back through your homework from last week. What one passage, key thought, or truth stuck out to you?

How have you seen and experienced the ways Jesus can mend even the most difficult relationships?

Discuss the cost of discipleship with your group. How do you keep Jesus first in your life?

CHICKENS
OR CHAMPIONS

REAL LIFE

This summer my precious sixteen-year-old nephew, John Michael, joined my mom Patti on a road trip from Florida to visit Missy and me in Tennessee. I think he was at least partly enticed on their *Driving-Miss-Daisy*-ish adventure by my enthusiastic descriptions of August in the Deep South; how one could outwit the afternoon heat by drinking sweet tea on a swing in the shade of a wraparound porch; how young couples often succumbed to the intoxicating perfume of jasmine and fell madly in love; or how evenings were filled with neon waves of fireflies whose flight patterns seemed perfectly synchronized with the frog choruses of nearby ponds.

> Can you describe a time when you've been baited into something that seemed so attractive that you just couldn't resist? How did it go?

Now those of you like me who have grits running through your veins, think Dolly Parton deserves to be on a dollar bill, and have a preference for men who drive big trucks and wear real jeans (not the skinny kind and never an above-the-ankle variation) know those romantic notions regarding the South are absolutely true—but they're only part of our summer experience. I didn't tell him that since we don't have the coastal breezes he's used to in Central Florida, sometimes the humidity gets so thick it feels like you're swimming in pea soup the second you step outside of an air-conditioned environment.

I forgot to warn him about the whole scorching-your-thighs-on-the-car-seat thing. I also neglected to mention that we have billions of mosquito bullies who punch the poor fireflies in the stomach, steal their lunch money, and then stab their pointy vampire probes into human skin leaving those of us silly enough to venture outside after sundown without being slathered in bug spray with gazillions of itchy welts. Lastly, I left out the teensy detail about how I was planning to coerce him into helping me clean out the chicken coop despite the you-could-fry-an-egg-on-the-sidewalk temperatures.

"Chicken coop?" you may be thinking with arched eyebrows.

Yes, a chicken coop because for a brief, regrettable moment I bought into all the hoopla about how raising chickens and collecting your own organic eggs would be healthy and fun. I went so far as to hire a carpenter to build a custom coop with miniature barn doors, individual laying boxes, and a hand-hewn ladder so the girls could access their newly fenced, free-range pasturette in style. I even hand-fed our seven persnickety rare breed birds dried worms as a special treat. That is until Missy (who I'd been thinking of when I started the whole hen hobby in the first place, assuming they'd be a sweet reminder of Haiti as well as provide an effective laboratory for hands-on learning) learned enough English to verbally express her disdain, "Mama, I do not like doze chee-kins … day stanky!"

She was right; they were. Out of the mouth of babes.

> When have you been left stunned and/or giggling in the wake of a child's politically incorrect but right-on-the-bullseye observation?

> What do you think Jesus meant when He spoke of the childlike requirement for entering the kingdom in Mark 10:13-15?

Therefore when Cookie, our galloping, typically gregarious rescue dog, "accidentally" ate one of the chickens after it flew over the coop, I didn't reprimand her too harshly. And when an especially shy one bit the dust after I'd chased off a homicidal yellow-tailed hawk I shed nary a tear. Just imagine me running uphill in pajamas waving a BB gun over my head and yelling, "Get outta here!" I suppose her wee, introverted chicken heart just couldn't handle the stress. Finally when the remaining five hens began scattering cautiously and clucking with disapproval every time I opened the gate to bring them more fresh fruit or dehydrated creepy-crawlies, I decided it was time for a separation between chick and state.

I could hardly believe the auspicious timing when my friend Heather—a recent collect-your-own-eggs-hoopla convert—called a few days later to ask my advice regarding what breeds were the best layers. I cleared my throat and proclaimed that while I grieved the idea of saying goodbye to our very own phenomenal layers (and they were, one of them—an Araucana—actually lay blue eggs), I might be willing to let her adopt them because my hectic travel schedule was limiting the amount of quality time I could spend with them. I did an internal happy dance when she swallowed my sales pitch and agreed to come pick up the feathery bane of my existence by the end of the week.

Which brings us back to John Michael, my darling kin who'd so innocently assumed a road trip to Tennessee with his feisty grandmother would be one of the highlights of his summer. The tender-hearted teenager who was completely clueless to the fact that his normally doting aunt was going to bribe him with both cash and Starbucks cards to help me clean fortified chicken poop off every surface our flock came within fifty feet of (if you haven't yet succumbed to the backyard fowl trend, beware, they are prolific poopers and will soil Every. Single. Thing. In. Their. Vicinity.).

Suffice it to say, John Michael and I ended up spending the better part of a scorching August afternoon hacking away at what I'll delicately describe as "chicken art" with every sharp tool I could find—shovels, screwdrivers, chisels, and a rusty post-hole digger. At one point of that terrible, horrible, no-good, very bad coop/shed/yard/tree/tin roof/lawn-mower/car cleaning day (I told you, they're prolific), my dear brother's son leaned heavily on a shovel and while mopping the sweat streaming down his face with the hem of his marching band T-shirt observed ruefully, "Aunt Lisa, I had no idea dried chicken poop had the consistency of cement. This stuff is so hard, it's almost impossible to work with."

For some reason his commentary tickled the two of us so much we ended up sprawled in the dirt laughing hysterically. But later on that night, after a very long, very hot, very soapy shower, I found myself ruminating about his observation. About how hard things are almost impossible to work with because they're unyielding, inflexible, and impenetrable. And then I couldn't help grinning because of the epiphany that I might just get to use the petrified texture of poultry manure as a Bible teaching metaphor!

What comes to mind when you think of the words unyielding, inflexible, and impenetrable?

When did you last get to work on an unpleasant task? Did you have any laughing side effects?

REAL TRUTH

At least 39 parables are found in the Synoptic Gospels of Matthew, Mark, and Luke (John doesn't include any parabolic text).[1]

Speaking of metaphors before we get to the hard part of the story, I want to take a little detour and talk about parables—the type of story we're about to unpack.

Jesus often told metaphor-laden parables to the crowds who gathered to listen to Him. Keep in mind, most people in first century culture were illiterate (typically only boys from relatively wealthy families had access to a formal education), which may be partly why the Good Shepherd shared stories common folks could relate to instead of making esoteric observations about Mosaic Law. The stories He told however were not for simpletons. They were instead more like a velvet sword or riddles with teeth. His messages packed such a punch they sent some people reeling. He used similes so compelling that others couldn't help but scoot closer to Jesus. Imagery so colorful it made even His disciples sit up straighter and listen in wide-eyed wonder.

I can only imagine the expressions of those who were leaning in and really listening to Him when He told this seaside story:

> Again he began to teach beside the sea. And a very large crowd gathered about him, so that he got into a boat and sat in it on the sea, and the whole crowd was beside the sea on the land. And he was teaching them many things in parables, and in his teaching he said to them: "Listen! Behold, a sower went out to sow. And as he sowed, some seed fell along the path, and the birds came and devoured it. Other seed fell on rocky ground, where it did not have much soil, and immediately it sprang up, since it had no depth of soil. And when the sun rose, it was scorched, and since it had no root, it withered away. Other seed fell among thorns, and the thorns grew up and choked it, and it yielded no grain. And other seeds fell into good soil and produced grain, growing up and increasing and yielding thirtyfold and sixtyfold and a hundredfold." And he said, "He who has ears to hear, let him hear."
> MARK 4:1-9

Jesus began and ended this sermon with the Greek verb *akouō*, which means "listen" and "hear."[2] So basically His homily is bracketed by the ancient version of that old-fashioned, albeit enthusiastic command, *Harken!* And the last full sentence our Savior concluded this parable with "He who has ears to hear, let him hear" probably had a similar effect on that original audience as a door slamming in a quiet house! In fancy seminary-speak that phrase is a Semitic idiom that emphasizes the need for careful thought and personal application (see also Matt. 11:15; 13:9,43; Luke 8:8; 14:35; Rev. 2:7,11,17,29; 3:6, 13,22; 13:9). It also may have been an implied reference to the Hebrew prayer, the Shema (Deut. 6:4), which means, "to hear so as to do."[3] In other words, put your money where your mouth is!

> If your closest friends and family were asked whether you were more of a "doer" or a "talker," what do you think the consensus would be? Why?

The use of *akouō* (ακούω in Greek) and its derivatives in the New Testament reflects something of the significance of the Word as it is spoken and as it is to be heard in the reciprocal New Testament relationship between God and man. The hearing of man represents correspondence to the revelation of the Word, and it is thus the essential form in which this divine revelation is appropriated.[4]

READ JAMES 2:14-26. How would you summarize the symbiotic biblical relationship between faith and deeds—between hearing and doing?

Now if you've retained anything from studying Greek mythology in high school or college, you might remember that the sense of sight was of primary importance in Greco-Roman circles and a lot of emphasis was placed on visual contemplation. So Jesus' emphasis on listening here in Mark 4 ran contrary to what was commonly espoused in ancient history. Therefore, based on His auditory emphasis, He wasn't trying to dazzle them by pulling a proverbial rabbit out of a hat but was instead trying to engage their hearts. The King of all kings essentially cupped His calloused hands around the easily distracted faces of His audience, turned them toward Him, and said, "Shhhhhh, stop looking around right now. Be still. Close your eyes and pay attention to what I'm saying to you."

> What distractions most often prevent you from paying attention to what God is saying to you through both His Spirit and His Word?

READ PSALM 46:10. What does "be still" look like when it's refracted through your personality?

What type of environment encourages you to be quiet enough in body, mind and spirit for your spiritual ears to perk up, ready to pick up the faintest signal from God? Are you able to access that kind of environment on a regular basis?

If not, what are some practical things you can do—to ensure more "be still and know" time for yourself? Feel free to enlist the opinions of your small group here because you know they've got 'em!

Are there any obvious squatters in your daily life who need to be evicted in order for you to hear from God more clearly and consistently? If so, what are they?

OK, now about those haughty religious poser types who dismiss parabolic literature as too simplistic. I beg to differ, especially since our Savior's closest companions and disciples pulled Him aside after He shared the parable of the soils and sheepishly asked, "Would You mind running that one by us again, Jesus, because we didn't really get it the first time?"

Later, when Jesus was alone, the twelve apostles and others asked Him about the stories. Jesus' response explains not only the parable but a primary reason for His use of parables.

READ MARK 4:11-20. Answer the following questions based on Jesus' response.

According to verse 12, how does the parable both reveal and conceal?

Why do you suppose Jesus would want to prevent some from understanding?

What did the sower sow (v.14)?

Who is the enemy of the sower/seed (v.15)?

What happened to the word in each of the four soils?
along the path:

the rocky ground:

among thorns:

on good ground:

How would you summarize the teaching of the parable?

The bottom line of Jesus' clarification of the parable is that hard hearts are resistant to the seed of the gospel, but it takes root and grows in soft hearts and leads to an exponential multiplication of divine grace. The moral of Christ's story is more or less what John Michael and I learned while cleaning up that hot chicken-induced mess: hard = difficult; soft = doable.

Read Mark 4:11 in two or three additional translations and then compare it with Luke 12:48. How would you paraphrase a believer's responsibility to live in such a way that her life reflects what she's learned about God?

1	2	3	4	5	6
so shallow they're poking up through the dirt				so deep, it'd take a backhoe to dig them out	

What would you describe as the common theme between Matthew 7:24-27 and Mark 4:1-20?

Describe the last time a tribulation or storm threatened your faith. Did your spiritual roots and foundation hold firm or did you find yourself pulled away from Jesus and shaken to the core of your beliefs? Explain.

REAL ACHE

The single most difficult thing Missy and I dealt with during the first few months we got to live under the same roof as mother and daughter wasn't her HIV+ status. It wasn't the frequent trips to the hospital or learning how and remembering to dispense her twice-daily dose of three different medications. It wasn't even my futile, scalp-torturing attempts to learn how to micro-braid her gorgeous Haitian hair. The most difficult, sometimes heart-wrenching, aspect of our first nose-to-nose season was learning to communicate.

On my five visits to Haiti during the adoption process, we'd managed to sort of understand each other with a few common words of Creole and English coupled with facial expressions and charades. I wasn't fully prepared for the frustration, anger, and heartache that would result from our communication gap once I finally got to bring her home to Tennessee.

The harsh reality of our communication gap became glaringly apparent just one night after we arrived at the Nashville airport from Port au Prince and waded into a celebratory sea of balloons and banners. I'd gotten her changed into pajamas and settled into her special pink and white Pottery Barn bedding and was singing a lullaby to help her go to sleep.

In the beginning Missy had a very hard time falling asleep. Adoption researchers and counselors say this is quite common. The busyness of daylight hours tends to medicate a newly adopted child's anxiety, but their deepest fears often rise to the surface when nighttime comes. Instead of becoming drowsy or even shushing me because my singing voice has been accused of being less than melodic, however, Missy got more and more agitated. So I picked her up and did several other things experts had advised me to do to demonstrate to her that she was safe and secure. But again, my actions only seemed to make things worse.

Finally, after more than an hour of her growing increasingly fearful and me vainly trying to sooth her, I went and got the Creole dictionary from the bookshelf and attempted to ask her if she was in pain. The second I began trying to articulate that foreign phrase her head snapped toward me, her brown eyes focused on mine with laser-like intensity, and she began talking as fast as she could.

A torrent of unfamiliar words poured from her mouth. After a minute or two, when she could tell by my expression that I didn't understand, she put both of her baby brown hands on the side of my face and began to speak very intently, with even more passion and volume.

Eventually I replied in English, "I'm so sorry baby, but I don't understand what you're saying." At which point she dropped her hands to her side, looked away from me with hopeless resignation, and began to sob uncontrollably.

All I could do was repeat one of the few Creole phrases I'd memorized, "Mwen regret sa. Mwen regret sa. Mwen regret sa." I'm sorry. I'm sorry. I'm sorry. My little girl cried herself to sleep her second night in Nashville. When her breathing finally settled into the rhythm of slumber, I walked out into the living room, sank into the couch, and cried until I didn't have any tears left either.

I felt like the precious daughter I'd longed for since I was a young woman and fought for through an arduous two-year adoption journey had tried to give me her heart, and I didn't have the hands to receive it. She threw a relational lifesaver in my direction with every ounce of her four-and-a-half-year-old might, and I missed it.

What followed were some long, heart-wrenching hours. My own dark night of the soul. And it's one of the main reasons one seemingly insignificant verse in Mark 4—which I'd read hundreds of times before without really noticing—now packs such an emotional wallop for me.

What did Jesus ask the disciples in Mark 4:13?

I think Jesus was trying to give them God's heart, and they didn't have hands to receive it. The situation not only reminds me of that horrible evening when I fumbled Missy's feelings, it reminds me of Paul's sober confession in 1 Corinthians.

For now we see in a mirror dimly, but then face to face. Now I know in part; then I shall know fully, even as I have been fully known.
1 CORINTHIANS 13:12

How does Paul describe our communication in 1 Corinthians 13:12?

Paul's divinely inspired and mercifully executed physical blinding on the road to Damascus enabled him to have clear spiritual vision. He realized that as created beings we will never be able to perfectly comprehend our Creator. Not while we're hobbled by humanity in our sin-damaged environment anyway.

READ ISAIAH 55:9. How would you paraphrase this passage so a child could understand the idea?

READ MATTHEW 13:10-17. How does this passage explain why Jesus purposely used the parables to reveal people's spiritual dullness (v.13)?

When someone in your past—like a boss or a personal trainer—has pointed out a weakness, were you inspired to work harder or discouraged to the point of quitting? Explain.

Not many experiences have been more precious than the moments of real connection Missy and I shared in the days and weeks after that terrible night of total incomprehension. I will never forget the first time we were lying next to each other in her narrow twin bed and she pointed to the shadows flickering across the ceiling and asked, "Iz at?" I quickly figured out she meant, "What is that?"

After I explained what it was, I thought I was going to levitate through the roof with joy when she chirped, "Dat's a SHA-DOE!" It was kind of like that famous water scene in the Helen Keller movie when Anne Sullivan swings open the door of Helen's dark prison.

I must admit, it grieved me when she stopped using her darling Creole-English hybrid phrase, "Oui ma'am" and replaced it with the accurate Southern girl affirmation, "Yes ma'am." (I felt actual sorrow, not the fake kind I exhibited when Heather finally toted those dirty birds away in a repurposed dog kennel!) But for the most part, the ah-ha look that lights up Missy's face fuels both of us with hopeful energy each time she learns a new English word or concept.

Missy's initial tiny steps of comprehension led to longer and longer leaps where she'd point to one thing after another asking, "Iz at?" "Iz at?" Then she'd giggle gleefully when she was able to correctly parrot my response. At the risk of bragging about her yet again, on the way home from school today she informed me that the apple trees in our backyard are "dizzid-you-and-us" because they lose their leaves in the winter. Mensa bound baby, Mensa bound.

But enough about my baby's burgeoning intellectual feats. Back to the valuable jewels we can mine from this awesome Bible passage. The delight of each new facet of knowing Jesus satisfies our souls in a way nothing else can. Because even more than Missy and I were made to be mother and daughter, you and I were made for deep connection with our Creator Redeemer!

Just like Missy and I keep wading into deeper and deeper parent/peanut waters, those spiritual ah-ha moments—when we actually grasp one of His promises or apply a scriptural principle to our lives—will lead us to pursue our Savior with more and more passion. Quite frankly, I believe when we taste even a tiny morsel of the communion with the God we were created for, we'll be ravenous for more!

> **READ PSALM 63:1-5.** If God's character was a dessert buffet, what would be your favorite item?

Enjoying a deeper connection with our Redeemer is why I'm also learning to appreciate the plow—whatever instrument God uses to keep the soil of our soul aerated and accessible to spiritual seeds—even when it hurts. And it will. Because when the steel of God's Word catches on a root of bitterness or becomes stuck on a stone of rebellion in our hearts, the dislodging process will be painful.

God's plow will likely leave a deep gash in our personal landscape. But it will also tender us toward His Spirit and help loosen our love for Him and others that we may not have even realized we were withholding. If you've put your hope and faith in Jesus Christ, the seed of the gospel will absolutely result in good fruit growing in your life. However, the size of our fruit depends on the softness of the soil. So how about it?

How tilled-up would you say your ground is right about now?

READ PSALM 119:75. How has God faithfully "plowed" you recently?

On a scale of 1-6—with 1 being a blueberry and 6 being a watermelon—how would you rate the size of spiritual fruit you're producing this season? Explain the context of your small, medium, large, and extra-large rating system (i.e. What spiritual action-reaction constitutes "large" fruit?).

1	2	3	4	5	6
blueberry					watermelon

READ MATTHEW 12:33 AND LUKE 6:44. How would your paraphrase these verses so that a child—or perhaps even an obtuse disciple—could understand them?

Jesus tags His initial farming metaphor with two more stories that underscore the necessity of hearing and responding in faith to God's revealed Word. He obviously knows His followers aren't the sharpest knives in the drawer—and that means you and me too. So Jesus reiterates the main points of the first parable to ensure their sieve-like brains could retain the concepts:

> Write your own paraphrase of each verse of Mark 4:21-29. Some of the ideas are challenging—didn't Jesus say they would be? So just briefly write what you think He's saying.
>
> 21
>
> 22
>
> 23
>
> 24
>
> 25
>
> 26
>
> 27
>
> 28
>
> 29
>
> In summary, what did Jesus say about a lamp?
>
>
>
> What did He say about a measure?

How is the kingdom of God like seed?

What do you think Ephesians 5:1-21 has in common with Mark 4:21-25?

"The parables make a direct appeal to the imagination and involve the hearers in the situation. This factor lends to the parable the character of an argument. It entices the hearers to judge the situation depicted, and then challenges them, directly or indirectly, to apply that judgment to themselves."[5]

The third parable Jesus used in chapter four (Mark 4:26-29) serves to clarify the first (Mark 4:1-9). It is the only parable unique to Mark's Gospel account, and it highlights the effective power of God's Word. God's Word is sovereignly sufficient to do His will whether we wield it or not! It reminds me of the strong word preached by one of my favorite long-gone-to-glory theologians, Charles Spurgeon, in a 1888 sermon entitled, "The Lover of God's Law Filled with Peace."

In the passage from Spurgeon, note the comparison of the lion and God's Word.

The Word of God can take care of itself, and will do so if we preach it, and cease defending it. See you that lion. They have caged him for his preservation; shut him up behind iron bars to secure him from his foes! See how a band of armed men have gathered together to protect the lion. What a clatter they make with their swords and spears! These mighty men are intent upon defending a lion. O fools, and slow of heart! Open that door! Let the lord of the forest come forth free. Who will dare to encounter him? What does he want with your guardian care? Let the pure gospel go forth in all its lion-like majesty, and it will soon clear its own way and ease itself of its adversaries.[6]

In light of Dr. Spurgeon's evocative word picture, what metaphor would you use to explain the awesome efficacy of the Bible?

"Basic to parabolic utterance is the recognition of the two strata of creation: the natural and the redemptive. Through parables Jesus called attention to what had previously been hidden in the redemptive order. The realism of His parables arises from the certainty that no mere analogy exists between the natural and redemptive order, but an inner affinity, because both strata originate in the purpose of God. That is why the Kingdom of God is intrinsically *like* the daily natural order and the life of men." [7]

Jesus lands His last parabolic punch of the day with a story about the miraculous multiplication power of God.

How does Jesus describe the growth of the kingdom of God in Mark 4:31-32?

According to Mark 4:33-34, to whom did Jesus speak only in parables?

But what did Jesus explain to His disciples?

I love that Jesus used a mustard seed—the smallest seed known and sown in agriculturally-oriented Israel—to illustrate the growth of God's kingdom. Coupled with Jesus' use of the mustard seed in Luke 17:6, it gives me—a woman whose faith sometimes shrinks to about that same dinky dimension—great hope.

Paraphrase in one sentence the parable of the mustard seed from Mark 4:30-32.

Paraphrase in one sentence the teaching that involved a mustard seed in Luke 17:6.

Did you write something like "God's kingdom starts so small you can hardly see it but grows to mighty proportions" for the parable? And the teaching says tiny faith can bring about giant results.

Here's a little extra credit to ponder. How do you think the two ways Jesus used the mustard seed relate? Do the two teachings somehow fit together?

Despite the seeming impossibility of the mustard seed metaphor, Jesus' words ring true in the marrow of my bones because I've lived them. In fact, I lived them last week when my dear friend Paige Greene and I were walking in a magnificent park here in Middle Tennessee called Radnor Lake.

Now just like the day John Michael and I developed a deep hatred for feathered fowl (see what I did there?), it was hot as blazes and uncomfortably humid. So by the time Paige and I made the turn back toward the parking lot, we were soaked with perspiration. But my steps were still bouncier than when we started our 4-mile jaunt because after I'd confessed a crooked place in my heart Paige had encouraged me by quoting a familiar passage:

> I thank my God every time I remember you. In all my prayers for all of you, I always pray with joy because of your partnership in the gospel from the first day until now, *being confident of this, that he who began a good work in you will carry it on to completion until the day of Christ Jesus.*
> PHILIPPIANS 1:3-6, NIV (EMPHASIS MINE)

Paige effectively reminded me once again that though sometimes I feel about as stable as a top-heavy Christmas tree in a stand with one screw, God will be faithful to complete what He began 40+ years ago when I gave my heart to Jesus.

Like me, do you sometimes need to be reminded that God's kingdom cannot be defeated in your life (Mark 4:30-32)? Share your thoughts.

Just about the time I was going to challenge Paige to race, since we only had about a quarter mile to go, I looked up to see a physician I've known for about twenty years. He was walking toward us with sadness etched across his face. He startled when he recognized me yet because I was feeling so grateful and so forgiven, I still greeted him with a smile and a cheery, "Well, hello Dr. Smith (not his real name)!" At which point, huge tears began rolling down his face.

Now it's not the first time a grown man has burst into tears in my presence, but thankfully his weeping had nothing to do with me being his blind date (not that that's ever happened before or anything). Instead, after we asked a few gentle questions, he explained that he was devastated over the death of his dad. It had caused a lot of soul searching, which eventually led to him questioning his own worth as a man. His broad shoulders and voice literally shook when he said, "I know God loves me and all, but when I look back over the course of my life, I don't feel like I've got anything significant to show for it. I'm afraid He's disappointed in me."

Largely because I was still floating on my own little cloud of revival, I looked directly into his eyes and asked boldly, "Dr. Smith, may we pray for you right now?" When he nodded in agreement (he probably didn't think he had much of a choice in the matter), Paige and I Went. To. Town! I mean we prayed heaven down on that dear man. All the while other hikers were walking passed wide-eyed and giving us a huge berth, Paige and I were bellowing God's promises with glad authority:

> For He created your inmost being, Dr. Smith! He knit you together
> in your mama's womb. You are fearfully and wonderfully made
> because God's works are wonderful—we know that full well.
> PSALM 139:13-14, RLV (RADNOR LAKE VERSION)

> Praise be to God and our Lord Jesus Christ! In His great mercy
> He's given you new birth, Dr. Smith, into a living hope through the
> resurrection of Jesus Christ from the dead, and into an inheritance that
> can never perish, spoil, or fade, even when it's super humid like today!
> 1 PETER 1:3-4, RLV

> God isn't unjust—He has not forgotten all the work
> you've done to share His love with your patients and
> other people in the medical community, Dr. Smith!
> HEBREWS 6:10, RLV

> With one glance of your eyes you captured His heart, Dr.
> Smith. The God of the Universe thinks you're the bomb!
> SONG OF SONGS 4:9, RLV

He's close to the broken-hearted, Dr. Smith. Especially on days like today when you feel crushed, you can count on God's presence.
PSALM 34:18, RLV

You can hold your head UP, Dr. Smith because there's now therefore no shame or condemnation for those of us who've put our hope in Jesus Christ!
ROMANS 8:1, RLV

I can't promise we weren't shouting a bit by the time we said "amen" but I can tell you Dr. Smith wasn't crying anymore. In fact, he looked gloriously stunned. Then his eyes got big and round and he said very slowly, "There's. A. Third. Hand." At which, a petite lady popped out from behind him and blurted, "I just had to stop and join y'all when I recognized Dr. Smith." She wasn't an angel—she was an acquaintance from the Chamber of Commerce he hadn't seen in fifteen years and didn't even know was a Christ-follower.

Out of all the numerous trails at Radnor Lake, three Jesus-loving sisters just happened to rendezvous at the exact same time and place when a brother had fallen to his knees after a swift kick from the enemy and needed help getting back up! You. Can't. Tell. Me. Our. God. Doesn't. Make. Majestic. Praiseworthy. Mountains. Out. Of. Mere. Mustard. Seeds!

> Does our Dr. Smith experience fit Jesus' promise that just a tiny bit of faith can move mountains? Why or why not?

When our faith wanes and seems as small as a mustard seed, we still don't have to live like chickens. We can hold our heads high and live like champions because of the omnipotent power and unrelenting proficiency of God our Father, Jesus Christ our Savior, and Holy Spirit our Comforter. Glory, hallelujah, and amen!

THE SOILS OF ISRAEL

The Lord promised Moses that Israel would discover "a land flowing with milk and honey" when they left Egypt (Ex. 3:8). This was good news for the herdsman and the gardener. After surviving the desert, the shepherds would find good pasture for grazing flocks in the Canaanite mountains. Fruit trees would be plentiful in a land known for its olives, figs, and dates, the raw materials for oil, sugar, and honey. But what about the farmer? Would this promised land provide the optimum environment for raising grain? Leaving Egypt behind, with its rich soil and natural irrigation, Israelite farmers expected to inherit "a land of milk and honey and bread."

"For the land that you are about to enter to occupy is not like the land of Egypt, from which you have come, where you sow your seed and irrigate by foot like a vegetable garden. But the land that you are crossing over to occupy is a land of hills and valleys, watered by rain from the sky" (Deut. 11:10-11).[8] Indeed, Canaan was not Egypt. Farming the "land of hills and valleys, watered by rain" was a risky business for the Israeli farmer. Without irrigation, farmers waited for the early rains in November to soften the parched ground, enabling them to sow the more productive winter crops of wheat and barley. The spring rainy season continued through April (Jer. 5:24), with the necessary rain to bring winter crops to maturation and fertilize summer crops planted in February. Standard amounts of deviation in rainfall varied from 20-60 percent due to meteorological and topographical conditions. Precipitation in the Judean highlands, accumulating up to 32 inches in a rainy year, surpassed rainfall in the valley for lower Galilee, which could only count on an average of 16 to 22 inches annually.[9] Due to the arid climate, three consecutive lean years of rain (above 30 percent deviation) insured crop failure (1 Kings 18:1).[10]

Farming the highlands was less risky than working the valleys. Highland farmers escaped the harmful effects of intense summer heat, which threatened crop maturation in the valley.[11] During the dry season (May to October), crops at higher elevations were nourished by heavy dew.[12] Furthermore, the Judean hills contain the desirable terra rossa, a very productive soil that derives from the decomposition of limestone bedrock. Shallow depths (less than 20 inches), however, make this soil susceptible to erosion, which highland farmers tried to overcome by terracing farm plants.[13] Weathered chalk and marl produced the rendzina soils of the foothills. Greater depths of rendzina soils insured soil conservation, yet high lime content contributed to their overall poor organic quality. The least favorable basaltic soils are more common in upper and lower Galilee. Basaltic soils run deep through

Adapted from "The Soils of Israel" by Rodney Reeves, *Biblical Illustrator*, Winter 1996, 56-60.

the plateaus of lower Galilee. Deriving from extinct volcanic activity, they contain minimal organic matter and large basalt boulders too huge to move.[14]

Jesus described typical farming practices of the Galilean in His parable of the sower and the soils (Matt. 13:1-9). Seed was sown by hand, scattered over plowed ground. Liberal amounts of seed would fall on a variety of soil conditions. With a second ploughing, most of the seed would then be sown into "good soil" (v.8), the deep basaltic soils that customarily supported grain crops. A good portion of the seed would fall on shallow ground covering the basalt rocks. Jesus' reference to the threat of scorching sun (v.6) may indicate a summer crop since winter crops were harvested by mid-May. Inevitably, some seed would be folded into ground harboring weeds, the perennial pest of all farmers. Some seed would even be lost on the footpaths that divided farm plots. Exposed seed was prime bird feed (v.4; see 6:26). Although Jesus did not include in his parable the essential element in successful farming—rain—His description of the sower and the soils conformed to common knowledge. He certainly did not paint an ideal picture of agrarian life in lower Galilee.

SESSION 3.
THE ONE WHO PREFERS OUR CHOPSTICKS TO BEETHOVEN

When Jesus calmed the storm, He spoke three words:
Peace! ____ _____! [see oh pa oh, fee mow] in Greek.

When Jesus calmed the storm, He demonstrated His absolute authority
over the _____ _____.

Jesus has authority over the _____ _____.

Jesus also has authority over _____.

The nature of her disease, an ongoing hemorrhage, rendered the woman
ceremonially _____.

The woman whom Jesus healed may have been _____ in _____
because she was afraid of being pointed out by someone in the crowd.

Sometimes religious superiority masquerades as _____ _____.

We all ache for someone to see us when we feel _____.

Video sessions available for purchase at
www.lifeway.com/GospelofMark

Discussion Questions:

What truths from God's Word came to light in your homework last week?

Discuss the authority Jesus has over the natural and supernatural world. How does that truth change the way we live today?

When have you felt invisible? What were the circumstances?

How can we reach out to those around us in tangible ways so they know they are not invisible and that Jesus cares for them?

THE SCANDAL OF A SCARCITY MENTALITY

WEEK THREE
Mark 6–8:30

REAL LIFE

Isn't this the carpenter, the son of Mary, and the brother
of James, Joses, Judas, and Simon? And aren't His sisters
here with us?" So they were offended by Him.
MARK 6:3, HCSB

The year was 1985 and I was a junior at Troy University in Alabama (I know, I'm not a spring chicken anymore). A summons on my dorm room door was from our sorority ethics committee. At first I thought one of my friends was playing a joke because all in all I was a pretty good girl. I mean aside from guiltily drinking a few wine coolers during a prodigal season and playing a tennis racket guitar a few times in an air band modeled after Blondie, I led a relatively tame life for a college co-ed. I even helped lead a Bible study in our chapter room once a week.

Then my roommate reminded me of the lengthy kiss I'd shared the night before with a darling boy named Bobby on the Sigma Alpha Epsilon dance floor. I knew I was in big trouble. Because within hours of giddily receiving our Kappa Delta pledge pins as underclassmen, we heard the rule regarding how a KD "lady" Never. Ever. Engaged. In. Untoward. Public. Displays. Of. Affection. communicated to us loud and clear.

The memory of a pledge-mate who'd been booted from the sorority the previous semester raced through my mind and I shuddered. She'd been caught in a more compromising position with her boyfriend even though she was a special "double legacy" (which meant two other women in her family history—in this case her mother and her grandmother—had also been Kappa Deltas). My palms began to sweat as I realized how leaning into Bobby's embrace (who I wasn't technically even dating at the time but who was oh-so-handsome) during an especially evocative Kool and The Gang song would surely be considered an incendiary infraction by a council of my Greek-girl peers.

A few hours later, I sat red-faced in front of four very prim, very proper senior sorority sisters. Three of them stared at me with deeply disappointed, pursed lips expressions, while the perky leader of the moral majority lectured me about how they no longer considered me a viable sorority presidential candidate because my unsanctioned public pucker had left a dark stain on my reputation and had scandalized our entire chapter.

OK, fast forward a bit. The year was 1999 and I had been invited to speak to a gathering of very conservative Christians. Mere minutes before the emcee introduced me, one of the women who'd organized the event pulled me aside and graciously, albeit nervously, asked me not to use the word "underwear" during my presentation. Which may seem like a strange request unless you've heard some of the colorful, self-deprecating anecdotes I tend to employ as spiritual segues!

Of course, since men were present at this particular event, I had no intention whatsoever of using the word *underwear* or anything else that could possibly be interpreted as off-color or inappropriate during my message. However her awkward request got me so flustered that the prohibited term got stuck at the forefront of my mind like one of those rebellious pieces of lint that keep coming back no matter how hard you try to flick it off.

Within moments of taking the stage I accidentally wove the word *underwear* into a sentence. Then in a panicky, stammering effort to apologize I blurted, "Please forgive me for saying the word *underwear* I don't know what got into me!"

A friend who worked for the ministry that sponsored this illustrious gathering of fine people (which shall remain nameless since I've already embarrassed them enough for one lifetime) later told me that my disastrous double misspeak pretty much scandalized their board of directors.

> I'm sure you don't blunder as thoroughly as I do, but how do you respond to embarrassments? Do you have a physical reaction? Maybe you look for some place to hide?

The year was 2013 and I was sitting on the front row at a large, national Christian women's conference during a CeCe Winan's concert. Now if you've ever had the sheer delight of hearing CeCe you know that she can flat sing. She's been revered for decades in the music industry and is often described as "The First Lady of Gospel Music." I think she's so anointed by God that angels stop what they're doing and lean over from heaven to listen every time she picks up a microphone.

Anyway, during the very last song of CeCe's concert I was so moved by the worshipful effect of the lyrics and the rich sound of her voice that I zipped off my black suede boots and hurled them onstage one at a time, which some of you know is a common response in traditionally urban and/or African American churches to an incredible performance. It's basically gospel music's version of a standing ovation. Flinging Cole Haan shoes toward the spotlight where CeCe stood was my way of saying, "GET IT, Girl! That's one of the most awesome ballads about Jesus I've heard in a long time!"

Unfortunately the arena security guards didn't interpret my actions quite the same way and several rushed toward me thinking I was a crazed, possibly dangerous fan who needed to be subdued. Thankfully I was standing near some of CeCe's support team who stepped between me and the keystone cops and persuaded them to put their stun guns away. Despite the withering looks I had to endure from some of her stiffer fans, who were downright disturbed by my behavior, CeCe found the whole incident hilarious and has teased me about it several times since.

Those are only a few of many stories on my "most embarrassing" list, so as you can imagine I was well-acquainted with the word *scandal* long before it became a popular television show. You probably also know the definition of *scandal* is: 1. A disgraceful or discreditable action, circumstance, etc. 2. An offense caused by a fault or misdeed. 3. Damage to reputation; public disgrace.[1] You may even know that our English word *scandal* comes from the Greek word *skandalizō*. But I'll bet you didn't know the very first time this word was used in the New Testament, it wasn't used to describe a prone-to-make-mistakes yahoo like me; it was used to describe Jesus!

> **READ MARK 6:1-6.** Can you pick out the English word used to translate *skandalizō* in Mark 6:1-3?

In your opinion, was Jesus the real scandal in this passage or should the people have been offended or upset at themselves?

Why do you suppose we find it so much easier to take offense and blame someone else rather than re-examine our own actions, attitudes, or beliefs?

How would you rate Jesus' response to the people in verse 4? Do you think Jesus:

□ accepted their offense and internalized it;

□ placed responsibility where it belonged;

□ sought to help them understand;

□ lashed out at them;

□ something else _____.

Jesus was not able to work any miracles there except to heal a few sick people by putting his hands on them. He was amazed at how many people had no faith.
MARK 6:5-6, NCV

Note the context of Jesus' low miracle count in His own hometown. The seeming failure wasn't His inability but His integrity; He refused to perform healings like magic tricks to convince a familiar, but hard-hearted audience of His deity. It wasn't that He "could not" but that He "would not."

Why do you think Jesus' friends and family in Nazareth were especially resistant to and completely scandalized by His ministry?

Luke 7:9 and Mark 6:6 are the only places in Scripture where Jesus is described as being "amazed." What amazed Jesus in Luke 7:9?

"Familiarity can blind us to the greatness and glory of a Savior if we are not careful. Spiritually inoculated at some point in life, we become immune to the real thing. I have seen it far too many times. We must not come to Jesus on our terms but on His. This prophet was without honor in His own hometown. We cannot make the same mistake in our own hearts. The consequences are eternal."[2]

What do you think it is about these two situations that caused Jesus' eyes to widen and holy brows to arch?

Think of a chapter in your walk of faith when you weren't outwardly feeling God's nearness and pleasure. How might Hebrews 11:6 address that time?

REAL TRUTH

One of the most familiar miracles—this and His resurrection are the only miracles recorded in all four Gospels—is the huge picnic made possible when one little boy's boxed lunch was miraculously multiplied after Jesus blessed it. But interestingly enough, that inspirational story about plenty is preceded by one about poverty. In this segment we'll work our way through chapter 6. We'll see tasks too big but a Lord who always measures up—and makes our little into enough.

> And he called his twelve disciples together and began sending
> them out two by two, giving them authority to cast out evil
> spirits. He told them to take nothing for their journey except a
> walking stick—no food, no traveler's bag, no money. He allowed
> them to wear sandals but not to take a change of clothes.
> "Wherever you go," he said, "stay in the same house until you
> leave town. But if any place refuses to welcome you or listen
> to you, shake its dust from your feet as you leave to show
> that you have abandoned those people to their fate."
> So the disciples went out, telling everyone they met to repent
> of their sins and turn to God. And they cast out many demons
> and healed many sick people, anointing them with olive oil.
> MARK 6:7-13, NLT

What teachings for your life do you see in Mark 6:7-13?

Verse 14 (NLT) says, "Herod Antipas, the king, soon heard about Jesus." Of course we can't be sure what he heard, but it seems that he heard of what the disciples were doing. It says, "because everyone was talking about him," but the context was the disciples' work.

How does the idea that Jesus' fame can be tied to our efforts affect you?

Jesus was becoming known to more and more people, in part because of the work of the disciples. As a result, people began to speculate about Jesus and the source of His power.

> What did the people propose as a source of Jesus' miracles according to Mark 6:14-15?

Mark used the idea that Jesus was John the Baptist raised from the dead—now that was some weird speculation—to fill in the back story. Mark relates how Herod reluctantly killed John (vv.16-29). Did you note those words in verse 20, "knowing that he was a good and holy man, he protected him" (NLT)?

Remind me not to depend on someone like Herod to keep me or mine safe. Read on in verses 21-29 to see how Herod cared more about the opinions of others than doing the right thing. Herod had painted himself into a corner, so to save his face, John's head had to go.

So while the Twelve were out there, sojourning all over Galilee without any material provisions for themselves, much less for the crowds of sick and poor people who approached them for help, they received word that John the Baptist, Jesus' first cousin and predecessor, had been murdered. I can only imagine how quickly the air hissed out of their evangelical balloons leaving them hot, sweaty, exhausted, disillusioned, and deflated. Surely most of their get-up-and-go had gotten up and left. They needed to come apart from the hustle and bustle of ministry before they came apart.

> How would you rate yourself on the busyness scale?
>
> | 1 | 2 | 3 | 4 | 5 | 6 |
> |---|---|---|---|---|---|
> | have to probe for a pulse | | | | running around cray-cray like your hair's on fire | |

> Are you as drained as I am by all these ups and downs? What did Jesus do when He heard their report in Mark 6:30-32?

Do not miss Jesus making a priority of rest. No wonder the disciples needed a nap. They'd faithfully completed their first mission trip and had complied with the uncomfortable, austere ground rules Jesus established before sending them off regarding not taking any extra food, or tents, or even a change of clothes.

What do you think the disciples learned from the experience of traveling without any extra provisions?

When did you last have to face a situation with less resources than you thought you had to have? How did it go? Did you learn anything from it?

READ PSALM 23. What do you think David meant when he wrote that the Shepherd "makes [us] lie down in green pastures"?

In light of your personal schedule this season, do you find yourself genuinely welcoming more ministry "opportunities" (e.g., baking a casserole for a sick friend or subbing in children's Sunday School even though you've already "done your turn" because they're short a few helpers) or secretly resenting them? Explain your answer.

As is so often true in our modern day lives, the disciples' respite didn't last nearly long enough because the stillness implied by Mark 6:32 was rudely interrupted by the clamor described in verse 33. Are you surprised that the situation reminds me of a story?

Missy was at a women's conference with me this past weekend. After a day and a half of being asked for hugs and to pose for pictures by dozens of well-meaning event attendees who feel connected to her through social media, she finally reached her limit. While sitting on the potty in the "family" restroom, yet another one of her fans chirped, "Is that Missy I hear in there?" outside the stall. My baby girl's big brown eyes searched mine pleadingly, and then she asked with a loud sigh, "Do I have to hug dat lady too, mama?"

Surely that's what the original twelve were feeling after having their first, much-needed, vacation cut mercilessly short by a bunch of paparazzi types who recognized their getaway boat and ran ahead to the marina to pounce on them the minute they pulled up to the dock. My guess is the band of disciples weren't feeling very hospitable when Jesus stopped and began to talk to the would-be stalkers:

> Jesus saw the huge crowd as he stepped from the boat, and he had compassion on them because they were like sheep without a shepherd. So he began teaching them many things.
>
> Late in the afternoon his disciples came to him and said, "This is a remote place, and it's already getting late. Send the crowds away so they can go to the nearby farms and villages and buy something to eat."
> MARK 6:34-36, NLT

In light of the disciples' state of exhaustion and the burden to deal with a needy crowd, their energy was in short supply. I understand why they encouraged Jesus to shoo the throngs away. These oh-so-human Christ-followers were understandably at the end of their emotional ropes. In addition, they were in the middle of nowhere with a noticeable scarcity of grocery stores and fast-food restaurants.

Have you ever been there? Ever felt like Jesus was asking you for millions when you were having a hard time even scaring up a little spare change?

It reminds me of 1 Kings 17:7-16. Elijah's landlord had a seemingly limited supply of oil, which was a basic necessity for survival in ancient culture. God miraculously replenished the oil Elijah needed.

> What basic necessities (i.e., time, money, food, energy) do you need God to replenish for you this season?

I have the tendency to run too long without refueling and run slap out of spiritual and emotional gas. I'm so glad Jesus didn't reprimand the disciples for their exasperated protest about sending the crowds away. Instead He gently pushed them a little further than they were used to going with the question, "What do you have that we can work with?"

> But Jesus answered, "You give them something to eat."
> They said to him, "We would all have to work a month to earn enough money to buy that much bread!" Jesus asked them, "How many loaves of bread do you have? Go and see."
> MARK 6:37-38A, NCV

The first medical mission trip I took to Haiti, shortly after I began the adoption process with Missy, was the single most overwhelming one I've ever been on. I've been to a lot of Third World countries over the years and have seen first-hand the heartbreaking effects of poverty, famine, human trafficking, and war. But I never got my hands super dirty for too long. Typically the trip organizer gave my counterparts and me short, pre-approved doses of the indigenous people we were hoping to assist. Then they would extricate us from the people's devastating reality and plop us back into a less dangerous environment—like a decent hotel after our brief allotted mission time.

But the Haitian trip had a very different itinerary. Hundreds of rural, impoverished people showed up outside our tin roofed pavilion on the first morning of the project. Many of them had walked all night when they heard the news about a free medical clinic at the base of a mountain. It quickly became an all-hands-on-deck, no-time-for-coddling situation in the sweltering heat. Since I don't have any legitimate medical experience, I was hustled over to the scabies/communicable skin disease/burn wound area.

The expression on my face must've conveyed my complete lack of medical training. The senior nurse who was running our little corner of chaos paused for a few seconds to grab my shoulder, look kindly into my eyes, and say with authoritative encouragement: "We don't have the medicine or supplies necessary to treat life-threatening wounds. We may lose some today, but bathe all of them. Put topical antibiotic on all of their wounds. Hold every baby, and comfort every mama. Just use what you have, and do the best you can."

Just use what you have, and do the best you can.

I think Jesus sent out the Twelve to learn that lesson.

The longer I run hard toward Jesus on this increasingly dark course called earth, the more I realize what sound advice that actually is. We must endeavor to bring the best we have to bear when it comes to loving well those He allows us to rub shoulders with. But we have to trust Him to provide the rest of what people around us need. We can't forget that when Jesus blesses it, even the most meager hors d'oeuvres can feed a multitude:

> When they found out, they said, "Five loaves and two fish." Then Jesus told his followers to have the people sit in groups on the green grass. So they sat in groups of fifty or a hundred. Jesus took the five loaves and two fish and, looking up to heaven, he thanked God for the food. He divided the bread and gave it to his followers for them to give to the people. Then he divided the two fish among them all. All the people ate and were satisfied. The followers filled twelve baskets with the leftover pieces of bread and fish. There were five thousand men who ate.
> MARK 6:38A-44, NCV

Mark describes the number of men in the first miraculous feeding as five thousand, which is a very imprecise census since the women and children weren't accounted for (although it was customary in ancient literature). If you include the wives and kids who surely outnumbered the men at this feast, "The Feeding of the Five Thousand" miracle would be more aptly titled, "The Feeding of Around Twenty-Thousand"![3]

The bottom line of this familiar story is: our scarcity + faith in Jesus = more than enough.

Compare 2 Kings 4:1-7 about Elisha (Elijah's successor) and another oil-challenged chick with the widow of Zarephath from 1 Kings 17:8-16. How would you synopsize the spiritual moral of both of their stories?

Mark 6:42 says, "All the people ate and were satisfied." How would you define being satisfied, spiritually-speaking? Are you satisfied that way?

REAL ACHE

Immediately after that supernatural feast of fish and chips Jesus provided, you'd think the prevailing mood would've been joyful, satiated gratitude. But the miraculous feeding only seemed to amplify the deep ache all around.

First Jesus' own disciples mistook Him for a ghost (Mark 6:45-52). Then the desperate hoards clamored for His help (Mark 6:52-56). The self-righteous Pharisees—so blind to divine grace, if it had been a snake it would've bitten them—prompted yet another verbal conflict (Mark 7:1-23). Finally we get to the part where Jesus seemed to be worn to a frazzle because He referred to a woman begging Him for help as if she were a dog (Mark 7:24-30).

What was wrong with the woman's daughter (Mark 7:24-25)?

What do you think you would be feeling if you were this mother?

How do you think you would have responded to Jesus' apparent insult?
- ☐ gotten angry
- ☐ slinked away in defeat
- ☐ called a lawyer
- ☐ given Him a piece of my mind
- ☐ other _____

Verse 26 tells us the woman was a Gentile. We often refer to her as the Syrophoenician woman. She begged Jesus to cast out the demon that was tormenting her daughter. Jesus' response almost takes our breath away.

How do you react to His response in verse 27? Does it seem out of character for Jesus? Why?

But she answered him, "Yes, Lord; yet even the dogs under the table eat the children's crumbs." And he said to her, "For this statement you may go your way; the demon has left your daughter." And she went home and found the child lying in bed and the demon gone.
MARK 7:28-30

Yikers. At first pass this passage sounds like Jesus is putting His foot further in His mouth than I did when I said that forbidden-foundational-garment word twice! But as is usually the case with Scripture, we need to dig a little deeper to discover the real intent and message behind these seemingly shocking semantics.

For starters, the fact that Jesus chose the region of Tyre and Sidon (modern day Lebanon) for a little R&R is telling. As best we can discern from the other Gospel accounts and historical documents, this is probably the only time Jesus ventured outside the borders of Israel. Which means it's likely the first and only time our Savior was surrounded by not only Gentiles/non-Jews, but by Gentiles who for centuries had been fiercely opposed to Yahweh and His people.

Secondly, the woman was Syrophoenician by birth—which means she's about as far removed from the spiritual genealogy apostle Paul referred to as "the citizenship of Israel" (Eph. 2:12, HCSB) as I am from Missy's biological DNA. So Jesus reminded the woman that His first calling was to enlighten the Israelites, the people group God the Father set aside as His very own. Then He probably winked at her when He said, "... for it is not right to take the children's bread and throw it to the dogs" (v.27) because the Greek word He used for *dogs* here is the diminutive term for a canine pet—like "puppy" in our vernacular—not the derogatory term used for stray or dangerous dogs.[4]

The woman obviously got our Savior's sly humor wrapped in yet another parable because instead of stomping off mad, sad, or seeking an attorney for a defamation lawsuit, this cheeky Gentile mama responded back in the context of His holy riddle: But she answered him, "Yes, Lord; yet even the dogs under the table eat the children's crumbs" (v.28).

I'm compelled to borrow one of Dr. Tim Keller's keen observation points because I think he sums up her persistence best, "There are cowards, there are regular people, there are heroes, and then there are parents. Parents are not really on the spectrum from cowardice to courage because if your child is in jeopardy, you simply do what it takes to save her."[5]

How do you think Keller's observation about parents could be applied to God's relationship with His children?

I tend to avoid direct confrontation with the same level of energy I employ to keep from becoming romantically involved with middle-aged, single men who live with their mothers or to keep from gazing in the mirror when I'm wearing Spanx®. Of course, I know respectful dispute is an integral part of healthy relationships—I had to pay a counselor $100 an hour for that cognitive awareness so I don't plan on forgetting it anytime soon—but that doesn't mean I enjoy confrontation.

However, if you'd been privy to the clear and concise rebuke I shared with a few folks in Haiti several years ago, you'd have thought I was a tough-as-nails trial lawyer. I found out they'd lost Missy's adoption paperwork for the umpteenth time without explanation. As a result, we were probably going to miss a government deadline, which would've then jeopardized our adoption. That could have lead to Missy's death because the medicine she was receiving for HIV and tuberculosis was directly connected to the legal guardianship I'd established.

I still don't *enjoy* direct confrontation, but if you threaten my cub, this massive mama bear rises up in my soul. That hairy chick will eat you for lunch and then calmly pick her teeth with your bones. That's exactly the kind of fiery persistence Jesus rewards the New Testament mama bear for in the above passage.

If you listen close enough you can also hear an echo of the same lesson He was trying to teach His disciples when He zapped an individual portion or two into a buffet bar that served upwards of twenty-thousand hungry festival-goers (Mark 6:38-42). He was teaching them to just use what you have, do the best you can, and trust Him to fill in the gaps. In other words, our scarcity + tenacious faith in Jesus really will = more than enough.

Don't miss that by healing the Syrophoenician woman's daughter, Jesus was demonstrating physically what He taught verbally elsewhere. For example, in Mark 7:1-23, He said what *comes out* of our hearts, not what goes in, makes us unclean.

For specific examples of things that make us spiritually unclean, see the chart on the next page. How does sin, or uncleanliness, display itself in your life?

Evil Thoughts	Evil devising and schemes. They set the stage for what follows.
Sexual Immorality (porneia)	General word identifying any and all sexual sins contrary to God's will. It includes premarital, extra-marital, and unnatural sexual behavior.
Theft	Stealing. Taking from another what is not yours. The eighth commandment (Ex. 20:15; Deut. 5:19).
Murder	Taking an innocent life. The sixth commandment (Exod. 20:13; Deut. 5:17).
Adultery	Violating the marriage covenant by engaging in sexual behavior mentally (Matt. 5:28) or physically with someone you are not married to. The seventh commandment (Ex. 20:14; Deut. 5:18).
Greed	Coveting, a desire for more at the expense or exploitation of another. The tenth commandment (Exod. 20:17; Deut. 5:21).
Evil Actions	Behavior that is bad, wicked; deliberate malice.
Deceit	Deception, dishonesty, cunning treachery.
Promiscuity	Unbridled, shameless living that is lacking in moral discernment or restraint.
Stinginess (lit. "an evil eye")	Figure of speech for envy, jealousy, rooted in unbelief. It believes God is withholding His best from you. A heart ailment that has the seeds of its own destruction sown within. It is never satisfied! It always wants more.
Blasphemy	Slander; defaming; speaking evil of man or God.
Pride	Arrogance, haughtiness.
Foolishness	Senselessness; spiritual insensitivity. [6]

READ 1 SAMUEL 16:7. How does this passage fit the Bible theme that God cares about faith more than pedigree?

I've often said Peter is the disciple I resonate with most. He talks a lot, stumbles a lot, and it usually takes him a lot longer than everybody else to understand and apply spiritual lessons. This may be part of the reason Mark's Gospel account (remember Peter's the one narrating these stories) is one of only two Gospels (with Matthew being the other one) that includes a second miraculous feeding. This time Jesus fed 4,000 men and their families.

READ MARK 8:1-9. What do you think Jesus was doing in His discussion with the Twelve in Mark 8:1-3?

What did their response in verse 4 indicate about their level of understanding?

Jesus was doing exactly what Deuteronomy 6:6-7 says. He was teaching as they went along. Obviously the disciples were, as usual, slow to understand.

What does comparing Mark 6:38 (with the feeding of the 5,000) and Mark 8:5 suggest to you about Jesus' patience?

What does this say to you when you beat yourself up because you've been slow to learn something or when you repeated something you vowed never to do again?

Jesus never ceases to amaze, does He? He took the loaves. He seated the crowd. Once again He gave thanks, fed the people, sent them home full, and had baskets left over

(vv. 6-9). Although certain people insist this second feeding miracle is a textual inaccuracy (these skeptics are probably the same yahoos who describe the parables as "simplistic"), clear differences in the details underscore the historical veracity of this story.

Not only did Mark accurately describe a second food multiplication miracle, he described yet another subsequent boat ride (Mark 8:10), confrontation with the Pharisees (Mark 8:11-13), and physical healing (Mark 8:27-29). All of these served as remedial lessons for Peter and led his noteworthy confession that vividly concludes the first half of Mark's Gospel account.

Who did the people think Jesus could be (see Mark 8:27-28)?

In verses 29-30, who did Peter declare Jesus to be?

One night a few weeks ago Missy quietly watched me pack the carry-on suitcase lying open on the bed for a few minutes. Then she looked at me pointedly and asked, "You goin' to work, Mama?" I replied, "I am, Honey. After I take you to school in the morning, I'm flying to Dallas for a women's event. But it's only for one night and I'll be back home the next day in time to pick you up from school." She considered my reply for a few seconds then looked up with a gleam in her eyes and an impish expression on her face and declared proudly, "You goin' to talk about Jebus, and God, and ME!" My little girl has been around me long enough to know exactly what I talk about whenever I have the undeserved privilege of a microphone. She has supreme confidence in knowing who I am and how I'm wired.

Supreme confidence.

Jesus had been called several names up to this point in the Gospel of Mark. At the very beginning Mark called Him "the Son of God" (1:1). Demons referred to Him as "the Holy One of God" (1:24), "the Son of God" (3:11), and "Son of the Most High God" (5:7). And while all those monikers are accurate, they somehow miss the mark (no pun intended). They have the same precise yet impersonal ring as when Missy accidentally called me "Lisa" the other day instead of "Mama." Those names adequately describe who Jesus is in relation to God the Father, but they don't begin to describe who He is in relation to sinners like us. Peter's answer is the only one that answers Jesus' question perfectly:

You are THE CHRIST. The Anointed One sent by God to rescue and redeem us into a right relationship with Him.

No question for humanity is more important than "Who is Jesus?" The only truly eternal scandal would be for us not to answer it exactly the way Peter did. Jesus is the Messiah, and He is our only hope.

Matthew 14:28-31 and Mark 6:45-52 both tell of Jesus' walking on the water. Mark's account, however, doesn't include Peter's attempt and subsequent sinking even though he's the one narrating the story.

Why do you think that is?

Have you ever tripped and fallen on your face right after a praiseworthy moment? If so, explain.

In Mark 8:30, Jesus "strictly charged them to tell no one about him." This is just one of numerous occasions in the first half of Mark's Gospel account where Jesus charged people not to tell anyone who He actually was. Often called "The Messianic Secret," it's generally taught He did so to ensure that He could move and minister freely until His appointed time to be unjustly accused and crucified in Jerusalem.

> What other reasons do you think Jesus could've had to counsel people to keep His true identity a secret?

The first half of Mark's Gospel account (culminating with Peter's confession in Mark 8:29) is all about the compassion of Jesus Christ, while the second half (Mark 8:31–16:8) is all about the passion of Jesus Christ—His unwavering commitment to fulfill His sacrificial calling of the cross.

JESUS' HEALING MINISTRY

"My Great Physician heals the sick...." thus proclaims joyfully a great hymn of faith.[7] Jesus has long been honored as the Great Physician. Twice Jesus referenced physicians while discussing His ministry (Luke 4:23; 5:31-32). These references and His pervasive healing ministry forever earned Jesus veneration as the Great Physician. Healing was such a crucial element of His earthly ministry that Jesus cannot be fully understood apart from it. Matthew explained Jesus' healing ministry by quoting Isaiah: "He himself took our weaknesses and carried our diseases" (Matt. 8:17, HCSB; see Isa. 53:4). Healing was anticipated in the Messiah's service, yet Jesus did not just marginally satisfy Isaiah's prophecy. Healing acts so saturated His ministry that any serious study of His message must consider His healing ministry.

The Gospels include 17 healing stories and 14 healing summaries.[8] They collectively testify that Jesus constantly healed people. This extensive healing ministry provided a context for Jesus' preaching. As He preached salvation; urged repentance; and proclaimed God's kingdom, compassion, and justice, Jesus healed every malady He faced. Jesus' healing was preaching in action, and it delivered a comprehensive message that might not have been believed otherwise. Matthew 4:23 states: "Jesus was going all over Galilee, teaching in their synagogues, preaching the good news of the kingdom, and healing every disease and sickness among the people" (HCSB). This and other statements underscore that preaching and healing were paired accompaniments in Jesus' ministry.[9] "Preaching and healing" accurately summarizes His ministry prior to the cross. Jesus' healing ministry revealed Jesus as being God and Messiah. Some healing stories record the people's amazement. Jesus' audiences realized God had entered their world with power. The amazed people reacted by glorifying God.

Clearly the Father meant to glorify Himself through His Son.

Jesus' continuous healing activity eventually induced deeper reflection. Certain individuals began to identify Jesus as the son of David—the Messiah—their Deliverer. With pleasant irony we notice that blind men desiring healing expressed this spiritual insight. Jesus' healings demonstrated God's power.[10] God's power shined through complete, instantaneous restorations. For example, Peter's mother-in-law immediately arose to serve her house guests. God's power conspicuously stood out as Jesus effortlessly handled numerous varieties of maladies for those who were blind, lame, deaf, or mute, or who suffered from seizures, palsy, blood disorders, leprosy, paralysis, and more. Repeatedly the Gospels profess that Jesus healed every disease. More astounding is Jesus' power to heal over distances. One story features a centurion who realized Jesus could heal his servant by an authoritative command without even going to his house.

Some healings became complex matters due to demonic entanglement. Nevertheless,

Adapted from "Jesus' Healing Ministry" by Mark R. Dunn, *Biblical Illustrator*, Winter 2009-2010, 22-26.

God's power was more than sufficient to over-rule the demons and cure the sick. Several summary passages associate healings and exorcisms, and five passages show Jesus dismissing evil spirits that caused physical maladies. Jesus' healings also convey God's message. After healing Peter's mother-in-law, Jesus healed many people, demonstrating that God sent His Son to minister to all people. Twice Matthew said Jesus healed out of compassion. The Lord's willingness to interact positively with people was proclaimed when a leper asked Jesus if He was willing to heal him and Jesus declared, "I am willing." [11]

Jesus claimed the right to judge religious practice when He deliberately healed on the Sabbath. Two such situations include the healing of a woman with an 18-year infirmity and the healing of a man with edema. Jesus further asserted His divine authority when He boldly forgave a paralytic prior to healing him. Furthermore, healing accompanied and illustrated Jesus' salvation message. Prior to feeding the 5,000, Jesus preached about God's kingdom while healing people. Elsewhere, Jesus healed while proclaiming justice to the nations. Jesus' healing, while motivated by compassion, was far more: it became "a sign of the arrival of the kingdom of God as promised in the scriptures." [12]

The proper response to God's message is faith. Jesus' healings carried an implicit challenge to believe. Many responded with amazement and belief. Countless people demonstrated faith by asking Jesus to heal. Some who observed Jesus' healings still refused to believe because Jesus did not conform to established religious authority. When some, as in Nazareth, rejected Jesus' authority, Jesus refused to continue healing. Still others boldly demanded "signs" proving Jesus' authority—thereby rejecting the "sign" of the healings they had witnessed. The great marvel of studying Jesus' healings is to watch the faith growth process. Faith drove some to approach Jesus for healing, such as the woman with the blood disorder and the blind men. Others were actually transitioning to faith, such as when a father who desired healing for his son, and yet declared his belief and begged for forgiveness for his unbelief.

Surveying the locations of Jesus' healing shows that most occurred during His Galilean ministry and many of those were centered on Capernaum. Some healings occurred as Jesus traveled to Jerusalem and some occurred in Jerusalem—even in the temple. Another way to appreciate Jesus' healing ministry is to examine the emphasis each Gospel places on healing. Matthew, Mark, and Luke saturate their accounts of Jesus' ministry with healings. Their passion narratives, though, do not mention Jesus healing any illnesses. John characteristically focuses on the dialogue of belief and unbelief, and famously only includes seven miracles. Yet three of the seven are healing stories. God designed Jesus' ministry to be saturated with miracles—as He was announcing and affirming His Son, our Savior. Healings comprised a large portion of these miracles, answering persistently Jeremiah's lament: "Is there no balm in Gilead? Is there no physician there? So why has the healing of my dear people not come about?" (8:22, HCSB). Yes! There is a balm in Gilead! The Great Physician has come. God's dear people are healed: the blind see, the lame walk, lepers are cleansed, and God's salvation has been proclaimed and demonstrated!

SESSION 4. THE UNLIKELY CATALYST OF UNBELIEF

The Mount of Transfiguration is on the northern shore of the ____ __
_____.

Theocracy: A people group God _____ _____ as His very own.

God appeared to His people tangibly in the form of a _____.

Jewish people call the glory of God Shekhinah, which means "The _____
_____ of God."

We need to acknowledge our spiritual _____.

"Helplessness, not _____, is the first step to accessing God."
Dr. Tim Keller

Video sessions available for purchase at
www.lifeway.com/GospelofMark

Discussion Questions:

As you hit the halfway point in this Bible study, what have you learned that will change your walk and relationship with Jesus?

We've focused on the compassion of Jesus so far in Mark's Gospel account. In what ways have you experienced the compassion of Christ in your life?

Discuss spiritual neediness with your group and reflect on the quote by Dr. Tim Keller, "Helplessness, not holiness, is the first step to accessing God." How can we be more vulnerable and honest with one another about our spiritual needs and helplessness?

GIVING UP THE "RIGHT" TO RIDE SHOTGUN

REAL LIFE

"Pride must die in you, or nothing of heaven can live in you."[1]
WILLIAM LAW

> How would you describe the drastic contrast between Jesus and His disciples in Mark 9:30-37?

Several years ago I had the honor and privilege of addressing a group of several hundred recovering addicts. Most of them were recovering from some type of substance abuse— like alcohol or drugs—and a few were recovering from various forms of sexual addiction and deviance. All of them were unflinchingly honest. And within a few hours, most of them seemed like old friends.

I've had an affinity for people in addiction recovery since I first began volunteering at homeless shelters with my Dad Harper when I was in high school. I couldn't quite put a finger on why I resonated with that particular people group until decades later when I was in seminary and read a book titled *Addictions: A Banquet in the Grave* by Dr. Edward T. Welch which includes the profound assertion and challenge that addictions are ultimately a disorder of worship. Will we worship ourselves and our own desires, or will we worship the true God?[2]

That's when it hit me: I'm a recovering addict too. Because the basic takeaway of Dr. Welch's book is that when we don't put Jesus in the deepest hole in our soul we instead attempt to fill it with people, substances, or behaviors. What's more, we are trying to fill the void God created for Christ alone. So while I've never struggled with an alcohol or drug addiction—therefore I've never lost my teeth to meth or been incarcerated on a possession with the intent to sell conviction—I did spend years emotionally imprisoned by the less obvious addictions. My drugs of choice were engaging in abusive romantic relationships and desperately trying to earn the approval of others. The consequences of my addictions weren't as outwardly devastating or illegal, but at the heart level they were still debilitating. And just like my now sober friends who were once addicted to crack, meth, alcohol, or hydrocodone, I too used to act like a sick puppy foolishly licking antifreeze off the garage floor, unaware it had the power to kill me.

Do you agree with the statement "All addictions are ultimately disorders of worship"? Why or why not?

Why are all addictions ultimately disorders of worship?

What did I have in common with addicts who practice more obviously damaging behaviors?

Who created the void we try so hard to fill?

Why did He do it?

Suffice it to say, getting to keynote at that conference for recovering addicts was for me like a peewee football player making it to the Superbowl. I was both thrilled and humbled. Although I didn't know just how humbling the experience would be until after I spoke and returned to my seat. That's when a woman approached without fanfare, knelt down by my feet, slipped off my shoes, gently cleaned them with a wet wipe, and then massaged them tenderly with oil from a small vial she pulled out of her tattered purse.

I've had my feet washed before as part of an organized group object lesson on servant leadership but that was different. That was a shared activity where all the participants knew each other and we all knew what to expect. Plus, we took turns so the humbling element was dissipated by the familiarity and the give-and-take. But no give and take buffered the impact of this time. I'd only met the foot-washing lady briefly that morning. To say it was awkward being the only person in a room of about five hundred other relative strangers having my feet coddled is putting it mildly.

I was so flustered at first I tried to pull my foot away from her, mumbling something about it being nice but not necessary. However, when she looked up kindly while holding my foot firmly and said, "Please let me do this for you." I swallowed the "I'm not worthy" shame erupting in my heart and yielded to her nurturing. Before long huge tears were rolling down my face because I was so overwhelmed by how she had minimized herself to minister to me. She was willing to appear subservient—smaller—so that I could receive care and attention. Her humble generosity meant more to me that day than I can even explain.

The next passage we're going to explore in Mark's magnificent Gospel account is all about humility. It's about how being willing to be less adds up to so much more in the economy of God.

> When it comes to humble acts of service—like washing someone's feet or washing someone's dishes who's bedridden with a serious illness—are you more comfortable being on the giving end or on the receiving end?

Why do you think you feel that way?

Mark 9:31 is the second of three passion predictions made by Jesus Christ; the first is found in Mark 8:31-32 and the last is found in Mark 10:32-34. The intended goal of these declarations seems to be to prepare Jesus' followers for His physical death on the cross and His bodily resurrection, but it was all too much for their finite minds to comprehend.

We are now smack in the middle of what some commentators refer to as Jesus' "Great Discipleship Discourse," in chapters 8-10.[3] In this section our Savior turns natural human behavior on its addicted-to-itself head and advocates a less egocentric, more other-centered way of living. He begins this particular recovery-from-self-absorption lesson with a reminder that His days as their Rabbi/Sponsor are numbered:

Why do you think Jesus repeatedly taught His disciples the message in Mark 9:30-32?

This reminds me of the time I spent about thirty minutes turning my house upside down while searching for my sunglasses. I grew more and more frustrated, only to have them fall off my head onto the floor when I bent over to look in yet another drawer. Jesus' followers' obtuseness was not altogether different from the Pharisees' blindness—and certainly no different from ours. When it came to understanding spiritual truths, His disciples often missed what was right in front of their faces.

Do you identify with Peter in Matthew 15:15-16? Looking back over the course of your relationship with Jesus, can you describe a couple of times when you were especially "dull" in understanding what He was trying to teach you?

Why do you think the same Greek word—*paradidōmi*, which means *to surrender*—is used in Mark 3:19, Luke 24:7, and Romans 8:32 to describe both Judas' yellow-bellied "betrayal" of Jesus and the way God sovereignly "delivered" Him up as a sacrifice for our sins?

How does living on the historical "already happened" side of that very first Easter give us an advantage when it comes to understanding Christ's teachings?

Of course it's one thing to be a dim bulb, but it's quite another to be argumentative and arrogant—which is exactly how the disciples were behaving as they hiked on to Capernaum, the next stop on their epic journey to Jerusalem:

> Jesus and his followers went to Capernaum. When they went into a house there, he asked them, "What were you arguing about on the road?" *But the followers did not answer*, because their argument on the road was about which one of them was the greatest.
> MARK 9:33-34, NCV (EMPHASIS MINE)

The highlighted phrase tickles me so much because I can totally picture that motley crew of grown men clamming up the way my six-year-old does when she knows she's done something wrong and might face discipline for her bad choice.

> **Me** (when I walk into my bathroom, which Missy prefers to hers, for the umpteenth time to find the toilet overflowing): Missy, honey, did you put a lot of toilet paper in the potty again?

> **Missy** (looks directly at me with wide eyes, feigning innocence): Hmmm?

> **Me** (head now tilted a few degrees to one side and emphasizing each syllable of the question with a noticeably lower voice): Did. You. Use. Too. Much. Toilet. Paper?

> **Missy** (now feigning interest in whatever's behind my head): . . .

Crickets. Nada. Nothing. Suddenly the proverbial cat has shoplifted my normally chatty daughter's tongue and she has NO WORDS!

Honestly, I don't know why I bother to ask. Unless we've been invaded by aliens, Missy and I are the only ones who have access to the commode in the master bedroom. So if it's been transformed into a waterfall again, giving me yet another chance to get up close and personal with our plumber (who by the way, really should give me a punch card because surely after nine visits the tenth one should be free), she's the darling culprit who caused it. However, my precious, Charmin®-loving peanut has already figured out it behooves her to plead the fifth.

Don't you wish we could see the expression on Jesus' face as He watched His disciples become mute, feign innocence, and pretend to be interested in whatever was behind His holy head? I can't wait to get to heaven and find out if my hunch is accurate because I'm convinced our Savior is a serial grinner! His good nature is implied by the way He doesn't rebuke them for their childish behavior but instead gently scoops up a nearby toddler to use as a living metaphor in a patient attempt to get His followers to—as we would say here in the South—act right!

Why do you think Jesus did what He did in Mark 9:35-37?

My guess is those burly men softened while watching their Lord and Savior playfully tease and affectionately cuddle a kid. Surely their defensive walls came tumbling down when He made eye contact with them while the child pulling on His beard, winked, then chided them gently saying, "I wish y'all would quit being so concerned about which one of you is the greatest and pay more attention to who's considered the least, like this little peanut right here who has no real standing or voice in this world."

You know the old adage, "Practice what you preach"? Well the following five, seemingly disconnected words:

Mom, Mama, Missy, Lisa, Harper

... are the result of what just happened while I was sitting at our kitchen table typing the end of the above paragraph. I'm in a bit of a hurry because this chapter is due to my editor by tomorrow so I've been sitting in this same spot for hours, too preoccupied to play with Missy. Which is why a few minutes ago she walked over, put her hand on my arm and asked sweetly, "Can I spell wid' chu, Mama?" And you better bet I scooped her right up and let her take over the keyboard! Good night, when it comes to God's slow-to-understand students who have to hear the same lesson multiple times in order to get it, I'm at the head of the class.

How would you paraphrase 1 Peter 5:6 so that a child could understand it?

READ PROVERBS 11:2. How has pride led to a literal painful stumble in your life? Taking the "painful pride quiz" below is a great way to assess where you are currently.[4]

1. Am I upset if I am not praised for my work?
2. Do I like and even long to sit at the head table in the seat of honor?
3. Do I seek credit for what others have done?
4. Do honorary titles pump me up?
5. Is popularity crucial to my sense of self-worth?
6. Am I a name-dropper of those I know (or pretend to know)?
7. Do I think I have something valuable to say about almost everything?

Now if you're a chick like me it may be tempting to generalize and ultimately dismiss some of the above questions as issues the males of our species struggle more with than the females. For instance, I couldn't care less about honorary titles. Years ago an accrediting institution offered to send me a formal certificate stipulating that I could now officially be referred to as "Chaplain" Harper based on some additional training I'd received after earning a masters in theological studies from seminary. When I demurred, they sent a follow up email asking what title I preferred to be addressed by. I never heard from them again after I sent back the reply, "Lisa." Some things just don't make it to our estrogen-soaked top-ten list. Unfortunately, in my experience, female self-centeredness tends to rear its ugly head in less aggressive, more subversive ways that can be hard to detect, much less root out.

What form of pride do you find most difficult to deal with in others?

In what ways does your pride most often show itself (or hide itself)?

A few weeks ago I had the misfortune of wounding the pride of a female acquaintance when I neglected to give her the shout-out she felt she deserved on social media. I only know this because she felt the need to share her disappointment with a mutual friend—after noticing an effusive public post I'd made about another person I dearly love—who then shared it with me. Mind you, I'd called and texted personal congratulatory messages to the offended girl, but nonetheless since I hadn't made the praise "public," she felt slighted. I think in women, pride often masquerades as insecurity, which may be less offensive initially than a boisterous, noticeably big ego but it's still fruit from the same self-focused tree. It's still all about us … it's just narcissism in a nicer outfit.

Speaking of being me-focused, I would be remiss if I didn't admit my own self-centered insecurity and shame. And while mine isn't typically tricked out of hiding by perceived slights on social media (which I think is way less than reliable if it's the only barometer you're using to gauge genuine relationship), it definitely makes itself known on a regular basis. Like when a man with whom I thought I had a real connection on our first blind date never called again. He told the person who'd set us up that he wasn't attracted to me or the fact that I came with the "baggage" of an HIV+ daughter.

The man's barb not only sent me reeling to the dark chocolate drawer, it convinced me to trudge down the path of self-pity. I wound up spending way too much emotional energy analyzing my unattractive parts (Missy not included—he was DEAD WRONG about her and is totally missing out. I may or may not have prayed for him to become infected with hives and recurring toenail fungus for dismissing my baby girl as "baggage.") and wondering what I could've done to be more alluring.

The bottom line is one less-than-flattering opinion about me from a balding man I only spent two hours with derailed my mind and heart from focusing on Jesus for at least ten times that many hours afterwards. That's the under-the-radar danger of pride-disguised-as-insecurity-in-women—it kidnaps us from living securely and abundantly based on the unconditional love Christ has lavished upon us, muffin top or not. Pride embezzles time and energy we could've used to attend to lost and broken people around us. It bleeds us of the peace Jesus died to provide, and it robs the world of the salt, light, and compassion His followers are called to display. Which must be why when asked what the three greatest characteristics of a Christian were, St. Augustine replied, "humility, humility, humility."

> What real life situations tend to provoke your pride-disguised-as-insecurity to come out and play?

Jesus used a real, albeit relatively helpless child as a living illustration of people who don't have much of a voice. Does anyone come to mind in your little corner of the world who would fit that description? If so, how are you intentionally engaging and encouraging them?

How does the encounter of Jesus and children in Mark 10:13-16 compare and contrast to the story in Mark 9:35-37?

REAL ACHE

Two incidents—one that happens immediately after Jesus' show-and-tell with a toddler and one that happens later on in chapter 10—reveal that despite His creative teaching methods, the disciples Still. Don't. Get. It:

> John said to him, "Teacher, we saw someone casting out demons in your name, and we tried to stop him, because he was not following us." But Jesus said, "Do not stop him, for no one who does a mighty work in my name will be able soon afterward to speak evil of me. For the one who is not against us is for us. For truly, I say to you, whoever gives you a cup of water to drink because you belong to Christ will by no means lose his reward."
> MARK 9:38-41

What do you think the disciples were concerned about in this instance?
- □ others wouldn't do it right
- □ others' incorrect doctrine
- □ credit going to others
- □ a decline in Jesus' popularity
- □ other _____

Once again instead of focusing on Jesus and following in His righteous footsteps, the disciples are preoccupied with who's right. And I think it's ironic that the group they were trying to incriminate had apparently actually succeeded at casting out demons, an activity they'd recently failed at because they forgot to pray (Mark 9:14-29). Goodness gracious, talk about pointing your finger at someone and having three pointing back at yourself.

One of the surest ways to discern someone's spiritual maturity is to listen to what they have to say about other believers who don't subscribe to every single jot and tittle of their theological doctrine. You can bet your bottom dollar that any Christ-follower who spends much time and energy castigating other Christ-followers is not spending enough time with Christ Himself. I think that bears repeating:

Any Christ-follower who spends much time and energy castigating other Christ-followers is not spending enough time with Christ Himself.

We should probably all cross-stitch that one and hang it on our wall.

Someone once said,

"World Missions is God's major therapy for our sin of
selfishness that eats the heart out of the local church."[5]

> You've probably also heard the phrase, "Christians shoot their
> wounded." Have you seen that happen in communities of faith you've
> been associated with or engaged in? If so, how did you respond to the
> figurative homicide or character assassination?

> Have you ever felt assassinated by a fellow believer(s)?
> If so, how did it feel and how did you respond in return?

> How does Philippians 1:12-18 underscore what Jesus said to the
> disciples in Mark 10:39-41?

Do you find it easy or awkward to cheer for Christians who are running toward Jesus in
lanes that are adjacent to yours instead of in your exact footsteps—in other words, do
you celebrate, support, and encourage Christ followers who subscribe to different biblical
doctrines or belong to other denominations, or do you tend to only mingle and tingle
with your own "kind"?

What is the line you will not cross when it comes to developing and/or maintaining
relationships with other professing Christians? For example, if you believe drinking alcohol
is a sin, do you still feel comfortable socializing with professing Christians who choose to
consume alcohol in moderate amounts? Or if you vehemently believe that it's our responsibility as Christ-followers to only vote for pro-life political candidates, would you still be
friends with professing Christians who don't share that same viewpoint?

A second incident proves how deep-rooted the disciples' me-addiction was. It revolves around James and John—"the thunder brothers"—who, along with Peter, were the three men closest to Jesus.

What would make you just a bit suspicious of the question in Mark 10:35?

When someone wants a positive answer before they ask the question, my caution flags begin to wave. Jesus asked, "What do you want me to do for you?" (v.36).

What do you think the request in verse 37 really meant? Why would it matter who gets to sit next to Jesus?

Here they are, several years into an itinerant world mission project led by Jesus. They've heard Him teach multiple times about meekness, servanthood, and how the last will be first. The Son of God has also soberly informed them three times by now (Mark 8:31-32; 9:31; 10:32-34) that He's soon going to be murdered in Jerusalem. Yet they're still so infected with a "What's in it for me?" mentality they can't stop fussing about who gets to ride shotgun.

Their presumptuous request probably relates back to His promise that the disciples would "sit on twelve thrones" with Him in heaven (Matt. 19:28). But these two prideful siblings foolishly laid an earthly template over Jesus' divine promise and were jockeying for the best position in Glory. My goodness, that'd be like if someone who lived under a bridge was graciously invited into a philanthropist's mansion for dinner but instead of displaying gratitude they plopped their grimy self down on a spotless, antique dining chair and demanded fresh-caught lobster as their first course.

What biblical context would you give to Psalm 37:4 when explaining it to a child or new believer to keep it from sounding like an excuse for entitlement (i.e., "God says He'll give me whatever I want!")?

Once again, Jesus took a different route than I would've. Instead of exclaiming, "REALLY, y'all" followed by a deep sigh and an eye roll, He exuded calm forbearance with those two knuckleheads:

> Jesus said, "You don't understand what you are asking. Can you drink
> the cup that I must drink? And can you be baptized with the same kind of
> baptism that I must go through?"
> They answered, "Yes, we can."
> Jesus said to them, "You will drink the same cup that I will drink, and
> you will be baptized with the same baptism that I must go through. But I
> cannot choose who will sit at my right or my left; those places belong to
> those for whom they have been prepared."
> When the other ten followers heard this, they began to be angry with
> James and John.
>
> MARK 10:38-41, NCV

Based on their immediate affirmative response to Jesus' questions, James and John were still operating in the dark. Had they actually understood the metaphor He was using for "cup" and "baptism" they would've at least hesitated before answering, more likely they would've panicked and sprinted in the opposite direction. Because the cup He was referring to here is the cup of God's wrath (Ps. 75:8; Isa. 51:17-23; Jer. 25:15-17; Ez. 23:28-34; Mark 14:36) and baptism is an inference to His imminent plunge into suffering and death (Ps. 69:2,15). Obviously, James and John would never have to face God's wrath because Jesus would accomplish perfect reconciliation with our Heavenly Father on the cross. However, when He asked, "Can you drink the cup that I must drink?" He was referring to the fact that both of them would go through incredible suffering for His sake in their futures. In other words, to drink this cup meant James and John were going to ache. They just had no idea how much it was going to hurt.

> How does James' ancient death (see Acts 12:1-2)—he was the first of
> the apostles to be martyred—compare to Christians who are being
> martyred across the modern world today?

> Do you think American Christians will ever face similar persecution or
> even execution? Why or why not?

John's "cup and baptism" included being exiled on the island of Patmos (see Rev. 1) as a result of the way his others-oriented passion for sharing the gospel blossomed after the death and resurrection of Jesus. And it was while on Patmos that he wrote the world-changing Book of Revelation, the caboose of God's enscripturated Word.

What difficult exile-type experience has brought out the best in you?

Some believe the other ten disciples were ticked at James and John (v.41) not because of their self-promotion or presumptuous attitudes but because they beat them to the punch. Whether that's the case or not, Jesus did settle their fractious brotherhood down with yet another lesson on minimizing ourselves so as to minister more effectively to others.

What do worldly rulers do according to Mark 10:42-45?

What did Jesus say His followers are to do?

What did Jesus come to do?

The world says, "Push to the front of the line!" Jesus says, "Go to the back of the line."

The world says, "Brand yourself and blast your accomplishments all over social media!" Jesus says, "If you want to be great you have to learn to serve."

The King of all kings laid down His scepter in Glory and came down to become man. Not a man from an impressive lineage, background, or position either. He chose to be born in a barn to an unwed teenaged girl, who soon married His stepdad, Joseph, who was a total blue-collar guy. He didn't just come to be like us so as to save some of us; He became like the least of us so as to save all of us. He is not an archetypal king. Instead of ruling from a castle, He had no place to lay His head at night. Instead of overseeing His kingdom from a throne carved of gold and inlaid with precious jewels, He chose to look out over mankind from a throne crafted from rough-hewn wooden crossbars. Plus, I've never heard of a regular ruler who proclaimed this as his mission statement:

> For even the Son of Man came not to be served but to serve, and to give his life as a ransom for many.
> MARK 10:45

Late great theologian and professor William Lane (1931-1999) is one of my favorite commentators on Mark, and he wrote this about the above verse, "The reversal of all human ideas of greatness and rank was achieved when Jesus came, not to be served, but to serve."[6] John Piper poignantly adds, "Mark 10:45 is what turns Christianity into a gospel."[7]

What kind of title would you give a king who embodies both of Daniel 7:13 and Isaiah 53:12?

How does 1 Peter 1:18-21 clarify or give color to the word *ransom* in Mark 10:45?

The word "ransom" implies an exchange had to be made to release someone from debt, slavery, imprisonment, etc. If you're a professing Christian, describe the biggest bars of the prison Jesus set you free from?

REAL HOPE

The night before I got to speak in the Saturday morning session of the addiction recovery conference I wrote about at the beginning of this week, I couldn't stop watching one particular woman during the musical worship part of the opening program. She was on the front row and she danced throughout every song. In light of the colorful backgrounds God had saved most of the attendees from, it was already more demonstrative than a typical Christian environment. But this woman was super demonstrative. She dipped and twirled with her eyes closed and her arms raised. Her countenance was radiant and she appeared totally unconcerned about whether or not someone might condemn her unrestricted behavior. I found myself thinking, "I'd love to know her story."

So I was thrilled when I walked into the church early the next morning and found her sitting by herself near the altar. I introduced myself and told her how much I appreciated her pure, unselfconscious worship the previous night. She seemed a little embarrassed, but mostly pleased, and went on to tell me her name was Joyce and God had indeed saved her from a nightmarish existence of booze and bad men. I could've listened to her all day long—not just because her story was so redemptive, but also because she narrated it in this wonderful, raspy, alto voice! I hugged her hard when the emcee walked toward the podium and whispered, "I hope we have more time to talk later!" before scurrying to my seat.

Moments later I took the stage and the title of my message, "Perfection Isn't a Prerequisite for Relationship with Jesus," was projected on the big screen behind me. Now because I like to be as close as possible to everybody when I'm teaching, I walked down the sanctuary steps while sharing an opening illustration. Then, when I turned to the biblical passage I was planning to expound on, I looked down and realized that not only had I drifted, but I was now standing directly in front of Joyce. So when a light bulb flashed in my tend-to-speak-before-I-think mind I blurted out, "This is my new friend Joyce, y'all, and she's got an awesome voice so I'm going to have her read the passage for us!"

Now please know I don't normally accost strangers and ask them to speak in public; I don't even ask my friends in our weekly Bible study to read out loud unless I've cleared it with them ahead of time. But for whatever reason my excitement trumped all reason and after enthusiastically introducing Joyce, I handed her my Bible, which was already opened to the relevant passage. Then I held the microphone up to her mouth and nodded and she began reading. After stumbling over a few hard Hebrew names in the first couple of verses, she got into a rhythm and recited the rest of the text with no problem at all. We grinned at each other when she finished, then everyone clapped politely and she sat down.

I didn't really notice Joyce again until I concluded the message and went back to my seat. That's when she approached me with a warm smile and a package of wet wipes. Yep, Joyce is the one who insisted on washing my feet.

When the conference was over, Joyce walked up to me and said, "Lisa, I need to talk to you about what happened when you asked me to read this morning." I thought, "Oh man, what have I done? She probably suffers from some latent public speaking trauma and will be scarred for life now." Joyce looked down at the floor and then declared, "When I told you Jesus saved me from alcoholism earlier, I didn't tell you how I fell off the wagon eight months ago and went and got drunk after thirteen years of sobriety." She then described how she'd turned back to liquor to medicate her pain and deep disappointment when the guy she'd been engaged to left her for another, younger woman.

Gesturing to the now empty sanctuary around us she continued, "I know you didn't know this church kicked me off the leadership team after I confessed my mistake." And she explained about how painful her dismissal had been. She said, "I don't really blame them for enforcing the rules and I know it was my fault and all but I did move my membership to another church after a few months because I felt like every time I walked in this place I had a big "A" for alcoholic on my chest."

Joyce went on to say, "And there's no way you could've known that reading in public has always terrified me." Then she shared heartbreaking details about her childhood that included not knowing her father and being largely neglected by her mother who conveniently "forgot" to send her to kindergarten. Which is why on the very first day of first grade, when a naive teacher called on her to read, Joyce stood up with knocking knees and sweaty palms and after several long, excruciating minutes mumbled something she hoped was somehow close to the written text she couldn't possibly read. Of course it wasn't, so the other kids laughed and called her, "stupid" a nickname that stuck through most of elementary and high school. She said from that day forward whenever she knew she was going to have to read out loud in front of anyone, she'd study the required text or speech for weeks ahead of time and would be nervous as a cat until the whole reading-in-public ordeal was over.

Joyce smiled when she told me that weekend was the first time she'd set foot back in her old church since she'd slunk out the back door almost two years previously after being reprimanded for drowning her sorrows in Jack Daniels. I cried like a baby after she exulted, "Today this place of disgrace became of place of honor because out of all these people you picked me. And even though I didn't pronounce everything perfectly, I still sensed God saying, 'That's MY girl!' the whole time I was reading."

"Those who've been forgiven much love much" is a familiar saying in Christian circles. It's based on the true story of a sinful woman who washed Jesus' feet with her tears and dried them with her hair in Luke's Gospel account (Luke 7:36-50). Based on my encounter with Joyce, my favorite modern day foot-tender, I think there should be a part B to that spiritual principle: *Those who never forget they've been forgiven much don't give two hoots about riding shotgun. They're just glad to get to be on the journey with Jesus!*

Which facet of Jesus—the Lion or the Lamb—are you more comfortable leaning into? Explain your answer.

READ PHILIPPIANS 2:1-11. In verse 5 the word *mind* can be loosely translated as "motive." What are two or three things that motivate you to love bigger, forgive faster, serve more sacrificially, and take offense less often?

In what capacity do you feel most comfortable serving other people? (e.g., tutoring at-risk kids; making hospital visits; inviting newcomers, singles, or those who don't have anywhere else to go to your home for Thanksgiving/Christmas; preparing for or cleaning up after an event at church; leading Bible studies; doing yard work for elderly shut-ins; etc.)

How are you living a life of service or how will you in the future?

DIVORCE IN FIRST CENTURY ISRAEL

Almost every extended family is touched by the heartbreak of divorce. The church should post multiple caution signs leading up to the cliff called "divorce." A strong guard rail and a high fence should be erected near the edge. But the church also should have an emergency vehicle waiting at the bottom of the cliff.

On one hand, our role is to teach and model wholesome, healthy marriages and to make it clear that God hates divorce (Mal. 2:16). On the other hand, our role as the church is to be a redemptive, healing community to minister to those who have been through the tragedy of divorce. After all, that is what Jesus did.

Jesus spoke candidly for God's intention of unity in marriage and spoke against divorce (Matt. 19: 4-9; Mark 10:11-12; Luke 16:18). Yet Jesus ministered compassionately to the woman caught in adultery (John 8) and to the woman who had five husbands (John 4). Jesus' compassion coupled with His strict views on divorce were contrary to the more common beliefs and practices of His day.

John the Baptist also held strict views of marital fidelity. He was openly critical of Herod Antipas for divorcing his wife and marrying Herodias. Herodias had previously been Herod's sister-in-law. John's public rebukes of Herod Antipas led to John's arrest and execution (Mark 6:14-29).

In Mark 10:2 and Matthew 19:3 Jesus' opponents tried to trick Jesus with their question about the permissibility of divorce. The test was twofold. Most of the people held that a man could divorce his wife for almost any cause.[8] If Jesus' more narrow views on divorce were known, He could have lost the support of many people. Also, since Jesus had moved to the region ruled by Herod Antipas, to have been against divorce would have been politically incorrect and dangerous.[9]

The Pharisees held two streams of thought concerning divorce. Those of the Shammai school interpreted "some indecency" (literally, "the nakedness of a thing") (Deut. 24:1, RSV) to mean that immoral sexual practice alone was reason for a man to divorce his wife. Those of the Hillel school stressed Deuteronomy 24:1, "she finds no favor in his eyes" to mean a man could divorce his wife for almost any reason, such as childlessness, a disagreeable attitude, or even if she spoiled a dish she cooked for him,[10] literally any "thing" that caused a wife to lose favor.

That Jesus was asked, "Is it lawful for a man to divorce his wife for any cause?" (Matt. 19:3; Mark 10:2) makes it evident that these Pharisees wanted to pigeonhole Jesus into either the Shammai or the Hillel way of thinking. "For any cause" was a catch phrase used in a raging debate between these two schools over divorce. That the debate was widespread probably meant that divorce was widespread also.

Adapted from "Divorced in First-Century Israel" by Bill Patterson, *Biblical Illustrator*, Spring 1998, 59-61.

Maybe even Shammai's followers did not always practice what they preached (Matt. 23:3-4). That divorce in the first-century Roman world was frequent is well-known. Probably, divorce on quite trivial grounds was not uncommon in first-century Israel either.[11]

Jesus refused to be straitjacketed into the common beliefs of His day. His answer shows He was at least as strict as the Shammaites, but His life shows He was not nearly as harsh or judgmental. Neither could He side with the lenient Hillel school. Jesus did not take His understanding of the issue from the Deuteronomic instructions Moses rendered "because of [their] hardness of heart" (Matt. 19:8). Rather, Jesus centered His answer on God's intention in creation Gen. 2. By focusing His answer on God's intent in creating man and woman, Jesus kept attention where it should be. Apparently, Jesus allowed divorce when the one-flesh union was already violated by *porneia*. The meaning of *porneia* is highly debated. It seems to be a general word for sexual immorality, including but not limited to adultery. In the case of *porneia* the Pharisees' view was that Moses "commanded" divorce (Matt. 19:7). Jesus replied that Moses "permitted" divorce, but from the beginning it was not this way (Matt. 19:8).

The union of husband and wife is so important that God makes the two become one flesh (Gen. 2:24; Matt. 19:5). That one-fleshness symbolizes a covenant relationship between God and Israel, between the Lord and His church (Eph. 5), and between husband and wife. Jesus' attention was not one "for what cause" a man can leave that covenant relationship. His focus was on its permanence and the importance of staying in that relationship.

Deuteronomy 24 protected a divorced woman by assuring that she would have a "certificate of divorce" and, therefore, could not be accused later of adultery if she remarried. Pink slip divorce or not, folks who have been through it frequently testify to the emotional ties they still have with the one they married. As a tree that bends around a rock stays bent when the rock is removed, so a divorced person maintains a bent of the soul where the other half of the one-flesh union once lived.

God hates divorce, not the victims of divorce. Divorce is not presented as the unforgivable sin in the New Testament. In fact, just before the discussion of divorce in Matthew 19, Jesus spoke of the necessity of forgiving others (Matt. 18:33).[12]

Jesus offered conversation, His Presence, and "living water" to an oft-divorced woman (John 4). This was different from the practices of His day, as the woman was ostracized by her own community. Jesus treated her with the dignity due every person created in God's image.

Like the woman at the well, many in our day, too, will heal from their painful divorces when we treat them with compassion and dignity. Many will yet drink freely from the "living water" (John 4:10).

Jesus held firmly to the standard of the permanence of marriage. Jesus also reached out with compassion to those who had known divorce. May we find strength to do likewise.

SESSION 5. CALLING ALL CURB SITTERS

The first chapters of the Book of Mark are all about the _____ of the Christ.

The last eight chapters of the Book of Mark are all about the _____ of the Christ.

Bartimaeus' saying, "Son of David" is a nod to _____ _____ that the Messiah would come from Davidic lineage.

In the first half of the Book of Mark, Jesus would often _____ those He healed.

The Greek word for rebuke, epitimyo, means "the implication of a _____."

Jesus wasn't asking about Bartimaeus' symptoms; He was giving him the gift of _____.

When Bartimaeus _____ with Jesus, he goes from sitting on the curb to _____ the cause.

Because of the compassion of Christ, it's _____ _____ Him to the passion of Christ!

Video sessions available for purchase at
www.lifeway.com/GospelofMark

Discussion Questions:

How would you explain the compassion of Christ discovered in the first chapters of Mark with an unbeliever?

How would you describe the passion of Jesus that is described in the last eight chapters of Mark and displayed on the cross?

Discuss the story of Bartimaeus with your group. What did you learn and how does his story compare with yours as you connect in a relationship with Jesus and follow Him?

THE BEGINNING OF HIS EARTHLY END

REAL LIFE

Several friends who've experienced both a miscarriage and a failed adoption tell me the emotional pain is not only intense but almost identical. They say it left the same cracks in their souls. They grieved both losses in a similar fashion, and it took them just as long afterwards to heal. Of course, I wouldn't presume to say my failed adoptions were as painful as the loss of the baby a mother felt growing in her womb, since I didn't get to experience the miraculous privilege of pregnancy. Furthermore, I don't think it's appropriate to "rank" grief.

I lost two little girls before Missy, however. One stayed with her biological mom and maternal grandparents. I know like I know my own name that was God's perfect plan for her. I believe He allowed me to intersect with their story simply to illuminate what choice they were supposed to make. Even though it stung a little, I encouraged and celebrated their decision to keep the baby.

Then the adoption agent I'd been working with for six months called almost four years ago now to tell me I wasn't going to bring the baby girl I'd already fallen in love with home. My heart collapsed as if someone had just drained all the blood out of it.

The call was actually the second I'd received from the adoption agent that day. The first time she called to let me know that everything was in place. She said the baby I was adopting was due in less than two weeks, and I needed to go ahead and arrange my flights because the birth mom had signed all the necessary paperwork. She said the birth mother continued to be steadfast in her desire for me to be the parent of her not-yet-born child.

The agent went on to describe how, rather than placing the baby in foster care when she was born, the birth mom's state of residence was officially giving them, so effectively me, temporary guardianship. The bio mom's blood work still revealed high levels of cocaine, and their state law prohibited biological moms with illegal drugs in their system from taking newborns home from the hospital.

All of this meant I was going to get to change my little girl's first diaper. I'd get to feed her the first bottle. I'd get to watch her sleep in the darling white bassinet with a canopy that my Aunt Darlene already had set up in their guest room for us. My agent then explained that we weren't allowed to come back home to Nashville until the final adoption paperwork was completed forty-eight hours after the baby's birth, but I thought, *No big deal. All I want to do is hold her … it doesn't matter where.*

After congratulating me and asking me to email my arrival itinerary as soon as possible, she said goodbye and I sank into the couch with a loud sigh. Pretty soon I was crying so hard with gratitude and relief that I had to put my head in my hands. Then before I knew it the sobs became interspersed with laughter. My shoulders shook and my nose ran and my heart did cartwheels around the living room cheering, *My baby girl is coming home! My baby girl is coming home!*

I was so joyfully discombobulated that I started praising the Lord too loud. I scared my poor dog! Then I started calling family and friends to babble the great news. A few minutes into the victory party, I heard the doorbell ring and opened it to find the UPS man standing there with a big box he needed me to sign for. After autographing his smart pad and giving him a much louder and more enthusiastic "thank you" than he was probably used to—I had to restrain myself to keep from hugging him—I plopped back down on the couch with another happy sigh. I gasped when I opened the box. I found the prettiest, white, faux fur receiving blanket I've ever seen.

It was one of the first baby presents I'd gotten because I'd warned my friends and family against getting their hopes up. I'd walked through a six-month ordeal alongside the birth mom—a precious prostitute with a hard-core crack addiction. I also asked them not to throw me a shower or buy any baby paraphernalia because the process was so precarious.

Those of us involved with the young woman's case were doing everything legally possible to help her escape the dangerous lifestyle she'd become entrenched in, but every step of the journey included seemingly insurmountable odds. It was nothing short of a miracle that both she and the baby were still alive by the end of her pregnancy.

When I pulled that gorgeous blanket out of the box and buried my nose in its soft folds, I thought the miracle was going to expand wide enough for me to become Anna Price's mom. The birth mother asked me to name the baby girl she was carrying. So I named her

Anna, after both my sister—Theresa Ann—and the elderly prophet Anna in Luke's Gospel account. She never gave up hoping she'd meet the baby Jesus. I combined the name Anna with my little brother—John Price.

Everything seemed to be working out perfectly. But then I got that second phone call from the adoption agency.

When I noticed their number flashing on my cell phone again I thought, "They probably just forgot to tell me about another form I need to sign or something," so I answered with a happy, "Hey, what do y'all need?" But as soon as I heard the tone of her reply, I knew something was wrong. Very wrong. I'm not at liberty to share the details, but due to circumstances beyond our control the bottom fell out of my dream to become Anna Price's mom. I didn't get to bring her home to Tennessee, and her biological mama didn't go to rehab. Nothing was wrapped up in a nice, neat bow at the end.

> I'm sure you have your times too—when events went from celebration to deep grief in an instant. Why do you think our loving God allows such times in our lives?

> What would you tell me of how God has helped you through such a time?

> What do you think God has taught you that you could have learned only through sorrow?

I was still reeling from devastation when the phone rang again an hour or so later. This time it was my mom calling on the way home from her surgeon's office. He'd just informed her the tumor in her abdomen was not only malignant, the cancer had metastasized to four major organs. He wanted to schedule surgery immediately, and his prognosis regarding her future health was sobering.

Later that evening Dad Harper called. By then I was so wrung out, so tired from crying and explaining to my innermost circle what happened, that I didn't have the energy to tell him about the failed adoption. I thought, I'll tell him about Anna Price and Mom tomorrow but right now I'm just going to keep the conversation short. So I asked casually, "How 'ya doin, Dad?" He paused for a couple of seconds, and then replied gruffly, "I'm not doing very well Honey because I went to the doctor this afternoon."

I asked anxiously, "What's wrong, Dad?" And he told me the doctor read the results of his latest scan which revealed the cancer they'd operated on twice before had now spread to his lungs and liver and there was nothing more they could do surgically. The doctor then informed Dad that he had about two months to live.

I prayed for my dad over the phone, told him I loved him very much, promised I'd call him the next morning after I talked to his oncologist myself, and then hung up the phone. I sat on my now dented couch for a long time afterwards in a state of disbelieving shock, completely stunned by the damage of the day. I wasn't sure what to do or where to turn. My mind felt sluggish and full, as if it couldn't digest another morsel of sadness.

> Why do you think the writer of Psalm 42 compared his thirst to a deer as opposed to a camel?

> When have you felt like asking God the questions in Psalm 42:11?

Scripture records many ancient leaders like Job, David, and Jeremiah weeping and even describes Jesus as crying over the spiritual blindness of Jerusalem (Luke 19:41-42).

> So why do you think Christ-followers often have a hard time admitting we're sad?

> **READ ISAIAH 49:11.** What metaphorical mountains in your life have yet to be turned into traversable roads?

Eventually, I went to bed and leaned over to robotically set the alarm for 4 A.M. because it vaguely occurred to me that I had an early flight the next morning. Then I remembered why. I was scheduled to speak to a group of ministry leaders in Kansas on the subject of "Trusting God in Difficult Times." It was supposed to be a message about how we can persevere because of the unwavering goodness of God. *Oh good night*, I thought. What in the world am I going to say tomorrow when all I want to do is pull the covers over my head and not come out for a long, long time?

All I had left was barely enough strength to lie down and breathe. Even then it felt like an elephant was sitting on my chest. Breathe in God's peace … exhale anxiety. Breathe in God's peace … exhale anxiety. Breathe in God's peace … exhale anxiety. Breathe in God's peace … exhale anxiety. After repeating that mantra instead of sleeping most of the night, the alarm went off, and I got up and walked into the bathroom and prayed. One step followed another after another after another until fifteen hours later I was standing on a stage in downtown Kansas City overlooking a sea of expectant faces.

After taking another deep breath to steady myself, I opened my Bible and began teaching about the sovereign mercy of God. About how His providence will never take us to a place where His grace is not sufficient. About how our Creator Redeemer is perfectly loving and faithful even when our dreams have been shattered into a million shards. And especially when we're so blinded by what's happening now that we can't begin to recognize His plans for wholeness and not for evil, to give us "a future and a hope" (Jer. 29:11).

How have you already seen the promise of Jeremiah 29:11-12 come true in your own story?

What does 2 Corinthians 1:3-4 promise about our sorrow?

When have you been able to use your past sorrow to help someone else navigate theirs?

As Jesus and His disciples turned the last corner and headed into Jerusalem for what would be the last week of His earthly life, His original twelve followers were walking into the greatest season of grief they'd ever known. However, their first "phone call" seemed pretty positive too.

What does Mark 11:1-11 describe? What do we usually call this event?

If you were one of the disciples watching Jesus ride into Jerusalem in triumph, how do you think you would have felt?
   □ Excited, Jesus is going to be celebrated;
   □ Amazed, others recognize Him as the Messiah;
   □ Proud to be associated with Him;
   □ Afraid, because Jesus had forecast His death;
   □ Other _____.

How much faith do you think the instructions in verses 2-3 required?

What life situation you currently face is challenging your trust in Jesus?

What do you think you'd have done when the people challenged the disciples in verse 5?

The fact that Jesus begins His descent toward the Holy City from the Mount of Olives is hugely significant. The mount rises dramatically, overlooking Jerusalem from less than a mile away. It's the same historic hill where Jesus later prophesied He would return a second time. Centuries before, Zechariah had predicted the second visit in detail. He wrote:

On that day he will stand on the Mount of Olives, east of
Jerusalem. The Mount of Olives will split in two, forming a deep
valley that runs east and west. Half the mountain will move
toward the north, and half will move toward the south. ... Then
the LORD my God will come and all the holy ones with him.
ZECHARIAH 14:4-5, NCV

What do you think of the form Jesus took for His triumphal entry
to Jerusalem? Why do you think it contrasted so radically from the
dramatic prediction of Zechariah?

I find the fact hugely significant that Jesus chose to humbly ride a donkey down that
olive-tree-dotted hillside. His actions were a dead giveaway that He had not come to be
the kind of military-minded king most Jews were hoping to receive. He would not defeat
their human oppressors and return Israel to its former geo-political glory. Rather, Jesus'
humble entry fulfilled another Old Testament prophecy also from Zechariah.

List every detail from Zechariah 9:9-12 that fits the way Jesus entered
Jerusalem.

What does Mark 11:11 tell you that Jesus did after entering Jerusalem
to a chorus of praise?

"Think for a moment, what Mark's record would convey to those who read it first—the Christians in Rome. No doubt many of them had seen generals enter Rome in triumph to receive the accolades of victory. How stark the contrast between Roman glory and Jesus' humility must have seemed. How mighty and powerful the sword and political power by contrast with King Jesus. Yet we know that His kingdom was established, while the glory of Rome disappeared into oblivion."[1]

How do you think you'd have reacted when Jesus didn't seize the moment and declare Himself?

☐ confused
☐ disappointed
☐ trusting
☐ impatient
☐ angry
☐ other _____

So while the disciples were basically clueless as to the redemptive drama that was about to unfold (despite having been told what was going to happen three times already by Jesus Himself!) every detail of the passion parade unfolded exactly according to God's plan.

How would you paraphrase Isaiah 42:16 and 45:2 into one simple principle?

About what danger does Proverbs 14:12 warn?

Have you ever charted your own course—confident that you were headed in the right direction—only to end up colliding with disaster? If so, what did you learn?

The crowd's shouts of "Hosanna" when Jesus entered Jerusalem literally meant, "Save, I pray!" and are loosely translated, "Lord, save us!" We see the same sentiment illustrated in 2 Kings 9:12-13 and Psalm 118:25-26. Unfortunately they were asking to be saved from their political/financial/social oppression, not from the eternally damning consequences of their sin.

> Have you ever begged God to save you from the wrong thing?
> If so, what were the circumstances and what did you learn from the experience?

The misdirected, noisy adulation of Jesus' entrance into Jerusalem soon faded. After a quick stop at the temple, He and the disciples headed to Bethany (where His dear friend Lazarus and his sisters, Mary and Martha, lived) to bed down for the evening. And the drama that accompanied His arrival took a very different turn the next day after an awkward breakfast fail:

> As they left Bethany the next day, he was hungry. Off in the distance he saw a fig tree in full leaf. He came up to it expecting to find something for breakfast, but found nothing but fig leaves. (It wasn't yet the season for figs.) He addressed the tree: "No one is going to eat fruit from you again—ever!" And his disciples overheard him.
> MARK 11:12-14, THE MESSAGE

Mark's narrative didn't note what expressions the disciples were wearing after eavesdropping on their Savior scolding a tree, but I imagine they gave each other sideways glances. They weren't used to Jesus dressing down a fruit tree. Maybe they even wondered aloud if skipping breakfast had made Him lightheaded. I mean, who in their right mind actually talks to inanimate objects, much less fusses at them?

Mark doesn't mention even one of the twelve asking Jesus why He's evidently so upset after cutting their eyes at each other, the ragtag band kept on trudging toward the holy city. However, Jesus' mood grew even darker when they arrived at the temple and found it transformed into a full-fledged flea market.

How does Mark 11:15-17 describe what Jesus did?

In our modern context, how do you think we can guard the purpose of our houses of worship?

What are some expressions of commerce that you think would be in keeping with the purpose of a Christian church?

What are some commercial endeavors you find disconcerting in a church environment?

Yikes! Talk about confrontational. When Jesus arrived at the temple He found the sanctity of His Father's house sullied by unscrupulous salesmen. He didn't hesitate to do some major housecleaning and sling some furniture around in the process! And it wasn't just because they'd desecrated God's dwelling place by turning it into a glorified mall. He was also incensed by the exorbitant prices the merchants were charging for animals to sacrifice. The arrangement made it impossible for the poor to participate in worship. That kind of crass capitalism got on Jesus' last nerve because He has a special place in His holy heart for the underprivileged.[2]

The confrontation escalated into a physical standoff when Jesus blocked those trying to traipse through the courts with their baskets of trinkets and wheelbarrows of caged pigeons and doves. The fact that His fellow Jewish countrymen were willing to violate the sacredness of the temple simply to have a convenient shortcut appalled Jesus. No wonder He turned on His heels and left Jerusalem soon afterwards.

Since the sacrificial system no longer exists, what modern day barriers have you observed—similar to the prohibitively high prices the money-lenders were charging for animals in Mark 11—that keep underprivileged people from worshiping?

In what ways is your church intentional about inclusivity? How about the women's group you're studying Mark with right now?

REAL ACHE

My guess is the disciples tip-toed around Jesus when they got back to Bethany that night because they were nervous about triggering another outburst. They were comfortable with Jesus extending gut-level compassion to lepers, sharing His lunch with huge, hungry crowds and hugging babies, but they weren't very familiar with this more intense side of the Messiah. I can only imagine their timidity on the breakfast run the following morning. When they hiked past the fig tree He'd cursed and discovered it was completely shriveled up:

> In the morning, walking along the road, they saw the fig tree, shriveled to a dry stick. Peter, remembering what had happened the previous day, said to him, "Rabbi, look—the fig tree you cursed is shriveled up!"
> MARK 11:20-21, THE MESSAGE

One of the most heart-breaking habits I had to help Missy break during the first few months after she came home was flinching when I raised my hand to fix her bow, straighten her collar, or caress her cheek. It was obvious that much like Cookie, our gentle and loyal adopted dog who was beaten by her previous owner, Missy had received enough blows in her past to create a deep-seated fear that surfaced whenever my hand got too close to her head or face.

Missy soon learned enough English to express what she was feeling when she ducked; she'd say, "Mama, dat big lady at da or-pan-idge hit me wite heeaw" and point to her face. The first time she said it, I picked her up and held her for a long time explaining softly over and over again that I would never, ever slap her in the face, hit her in the head, or intentionally hurt her. Once she finally relaxed and fell asleep in my arms, I laid her on the bed, pulled the covers up around her, walked out into the living room, and cried.

> When has a situation caused you to weep till you thought you had no more tears left?

READ LUKE 19:41-44. How do you identify with the sorrow Jesus expressed in this passage?

I'll never forget the look of terror that washed over Missy's face when she thought I was going to strike her. Or the angst of realizing that sometimes she was afraid of me. I can't help wondering since Jesus was God incarnate—perfectly God and perfectly human—if He grieved the disciple's distorted view of Him too. Their understanding of who He was obviously mattered to Him or He wouldn't have attempted to explain His death and resurrection to them multiple times, much less ask them, "But who do you say that I am?" (Mark 8:29).

Years ago I was sitting in my counselor's office when she explained that one of the most common heartaches she hears is: "I just wish someone understood me." She said the core of many of our emotional wounds is the pain of feeling missed or misunderstood.

Thus far we've focused on us in the "Real Ache" section of this Bible study, but now let's turn our attention to Jesus. Do you think it's possible that He ached over being missed and misunderstood by His closest companions? Do you think He ached when people minimized His deity by essentially asking Him to perform tricks like a traveling magician (John 6:30-31)? How about when He was slandered, vilified, and set up for murder by the religious leaders of His day? The very men denied Him who made a living poring over and preaching the Old Testament—which was all about Him (Luke 24:27).

It broke my heart to be misunderstood by my little girl for just a few months. I can't begin to imagine the agony of being misunderstood by the entire world for whom you'd come to lay down your life.

How does that rejection of Jesus continue to this day?

READ JOHN 3:18-20. What does John indicate about our tendency to reject the identity of Jesus?

The Bible describes at least twenty distinct emotions that Jesus expressed during His earthly ministry. He showed affection, anguish, anger, compassion, distress, grief, gladness, indignation, joy, love, peace, sadness, sympathy, agitation, and exhaustion.

Which of Jesus' emotions is the most difficult for you to imagine Him feeling? Explain your answer.

The phrase "Analogy of Scripture" refers to using the entirety of God's Word to interpret a particular Scripture; the scope and significance of one passage is better understood by relating it to others. The Westminster Confession explains this principle further: "The infallible rule of interpretation of Scripture is the Scripture itself: and therefore, when there is a question about the true and full sense of any Scripture (which is not manifold, but one), it must be searched and known by other places that speak more clearly."[3]

Think of the most painful or humiliating experience you've ever walked through. Can you imagine Jesus walking there before you?

How does Hebrews 4:14-16 change your perception of that experience?

What do you feel when you picture Him there prior to you, praying for you in the place you'd most like to forget?

Harry Nilsson wrote a song called "One" which went on to reach #5 on the Billboard Hot 100 list when it was recorded in 1969 by the band Three Dog Night. It included the lyrics, "One is the loneliest number that you'll ever do. ... It's the loneliest number since the number one."[4]

Which number do you think is lonelier, one or two? Why?

How do the lyrics of Psalm 139 refute the rampant human emotion of not feeling "known"?

REAL HOPE

Jesus appeared to be in a foul mood when He lambasted that fig tree for the seemingly minor infraction of having no fruit. After all, it wasn't even in season. This tree-zapping incident represents a lot more than simply the Savior's growling stomach.

> Have you encountered things in Scripture that seemed harsh or even wrong until you learned more about the context? If so, describe one or more examples.

The fig tree often symbolized Israel's relationship with God in the Old Testament (Jer. 8:13; Hos. 9:10,16; Joel 1:7; Mic. 4:3-4; Zech. 3:10). Fig trees were also used as a symbol of peace and prosperity (1 Kings 4:25). And a "poultice of figs" was the prescription Isaiah used to cure King Hezekiah's life-threatening illness (2 Kings 20:7, NIV).

How have you come to reconcile these problematic passages?

Common examples you could have cited include the flood in Noah's day in Genesis 6–7, the destruction of the firstborn in Egypt in Exodus 11:5, or the order to eliminate the Canaanites in Deuteronomy 20:17. Sometimes Scripture records harsh judgments that our soft hearts don't want to consider. These constitute another study entirely, but just let me note that when we understand the larger context we can better appreciate the holiness and goodness of God.

In the case of Jesus cursing the fig tree, the message begins to crystallize when we consider this took place during the spring, when fig trees sport both foliage and a crop of small knobs the size of almonds (called *taqsh* in Palestinian Arabic), which are forerunners to the real figs that appear about six weeks later.[5] Therefore when Jesus found "nothing but leaves" (Mark 11:13), He knew this particular nub-less perennial would never bear fruit and was therefore useless.

So Jesus wasn't simply protesting unproductive vegetation; He was using the fruitless tree as a prophetic symbol for Israel's hypocrisy. God's chosen people had stopped producing the real fruit of relationship with Him through prayer and worship and were instead engaged in the ostentatious but spiritually barren practice of ritual and legalism. By killing

Matthew 13:55 and Mark 6:3 imply that Jesus apprenticed with His stepfather Joseph as a *tektón*, which most English Bibles translate as "carpenter." However, the literal definition of that Greek word *tektón* is actually broader and is better translated as "builder."[6] Which brings to mind a much beefier mental image of Jesus than the slender blonde-guy-with-a-tepid-expression that ancient artists favored. Most of the general contractors I've met have the muscles and the moxie to clear a room just like Jesus did when He found His Father's house full of profiteering scoundrels!

a showy yet sterile tree, Jesus was making the emphatic point that our Creator will not allow unrepentant sinners masquerading as spiritual folks to flourish indefinitely.

And when Peter nervously pointed out the withered shrub, Jesus stopped and took the time to reassure His disciples of their favored position as the family of God. Not altogether different than when I promised Missy that I would never intentionally hurt her:

Then Jesus said to the disciples, "Have faith in God. I tell you the truth, you can say to this mountain, 'May you be lifted up and thrown into the sea,' and it will happen. But you must really believe it will happen and have no doubt in your heart. I tell you, you can pray for anything, and if you believe that you've received it, it will be yours. But when you are praying, first forgive anyone you are holding a grudge against, so that your Father in heaven will forgive your sins, too."
MARK 11:22-25, NLT

Speaking of special perks that come when you're part of God's family, this passage in Mark reminds me so much of a parable in Luke. The parable of the friend at midnight also revolves around prayer.

How would you summarize in a sentence or two what Jesus was teaching in Luke 11:5-13?

I've heard Sunday School teachers focus on the neighbor's persistence in this parable. They emphasized how we need to be just as relentless in our prayer life. The problem with that perspective is the implication that God is a supernatural sleepyhead who's reluctant to rouse Himself and answer our cries for help. Numerous descriptions of God's compassion throughout Scripture refute that idea.

The priceless treasure in this divine tale is actually the proximity of the children to their father. The point of the parable is contrast ("how much more," v.13). It illustrates how we don't have to beg to get God's attention or twist His arm to get Him to act on our behalf. Instead He hears our faintest whispers because we're under His roof so to speak, plus we can freely ask Him for anything because He's the kind of dad who absolutely adores His children!

Jesus wrapped almost exactly the same promise around His anxious followers after the fig tree fizzle and shortly before facing the cross. It was the beginning of His earthly end, yet the Lord of all still took the time to calm His friends' fears with the reminder that they could approach the throne of God with confidence because they were now considered family. Once again He perfectly practiced what He preached—"For even the Son of Man came not to be served but to serve, and to give his life as a ransom for many" (Mark 10:45). In so doing Jesus made that motley crew of often obtuse disciples feel completely known, loved, and valued. Wow, talk about relieving an ache!

REREAD MARK 11:22-26. What spiritual principles does this passage contain regarding prayer and faith?

How would you describe the difference between an unhealthy "name it and claim it" doctrine and the type of faithful prayer posture Jesus advocates here in Mark 11?

TEMPLE MERCHANTS

The priests were puzzled by Jesus' radical activity in the temple. They were both outraged and curious about why this new teacher was behaving in a way that seemed more typical of a prophet like John the Baptist. They rightly wanted to know the meaning of Jesus' obvious indignation.

Jesus was displaying God's indignation for the commercialization of His holy temple. The Gospel of John indicates that He was also fulfilling a messianic prophecy. God was displeased with the commercialism and profiteering of unscrupulous temple merchants. But who were those merchants who were the object of His indignation? Why were they in the temple area to begin with?

The daily sacrifice, offered morning and evening, was the central event in temple life. The sacrifice involved a lengthy and imposing ceremony that followed a detailed ritual. Feast days and the Sabbath meant additional sacrifices and even more elaborate ceremonial rituals.[7]

The temple merchants were sellers of livestock and other items to be sacrificed in the temple. Sacrificed animals had to be unblemished (see Lev. 22:17-25). Diseased, injured, or castrated animals were unacceptable. The only kinds of animals that could be offered were cattle, sheep, goats, doves, and pigeons. Vegetable offerings from the harvest of the land were also offered.

In the outer courts with the merchants who sold animals, birds, and other items, there were also currency exchangers who provided acceptable currency for offerings in the temple. In New Testament times cities issued their own money. Coins differed from

country to country, so equivalents had to be worked out by the money changers. The money changers exchanged Roman money for the Tyrian shekel, which was required for the annual temple tax that was imposed on all Jewish males (see Ex. 30:11-16). This coin was the nearest available equivalent to the Old Testament shekel.[8]

Because Jews from various countries who came to pay the temple tax brought various types of coinage, temple authorities had to authorize a particular coin for the purpose. The coin they authorized was the silver Tyrian half-shekel, or tetradrachma. According to the Mishna (Sheqalim 1:3) the money changers collected this tax in the provinces on the 15th of the month of Adar (the month before the Passover). Ten days before the Passover they moved to the temple courts, where they assisted Jews from foreign countries who needed to procure the half-shekel to pay their tax. But these worshipers also needed to purchase birds, animals, or cake offerings.[9]

For the convenience of the numerous worshipers, especially those from foreign countries, the money changers and vendors had been allowed to set up their tables in the court of the Gentiles or outer court. This resulted in a great deal of haggling, and even dishonesty, in the outer court. The annual temple tax and the constant

Adapted from "Temple Merchants" by James E. Finch, *Biblical Illustrator*, Winter 1995, 59-60.

giving of offerings gave the money changers and sellers of animals and other items the opportunity to profit from providing pilgrims and natives the items needed for the offerings being made in the temple.

The offerings were numerous and of various kinds. There was a daily demand for cereal grains and sacrificial animals. The more prosperous individuals offered animals, and the poor offered cereals.

The money changer served as a financier and banker, often sitting at the gate of the city or the temple to perform the exchanges required for commerce. When a money changer exchanged silver Tyrian tetradrachmas for local shekels, a fee was exacted. Money changers sometimes cheated when assisting in transactions involving the sale of sacrificial animals.

The temple money changers also loaned money, sometimes charging as much as 300 percent interest.[10] They carried out many of the activities associated with present-day bankers, but with fewer controls by the temple and the government.

Christ denounced the money changers because their excessively high rates for exchanging the currency brought in by Jews from other nations.

The stricter Jews complained that the temple was being used as a thoroughfare and that trivial transactions were taking place on the threshold of God's house.

Why did the merchants bear the brunt of Jesus' anger? Jesus was demonstrating God's displeasure with the commercialism that had grown up around the temple. He possibly was being indignant about the profits being made, legally and illegally, from the pilgrims who were coming to the temple to worship.

No doubt, He also was demonstrating anger about the laxness of the temple priests and the religious establishment. The priestly hierarchy was a family affair at the top and was obviously political and commercial in many of its concerns. The fact that the holiness of the temple would be compromised for commercial purposes was an indictment against the religious rulers of the nation.

The trading was being conducted in the court of the Gentiles. Jesus' action was possibly a reaction against the commercialism that apparently shut the Gentiles out of the one place they were supposed to be allowed to worship God.

Jesus' position was consistent with the teachings of the rabbis: "What is the reverence of the Temple? That none go into the Mountain of the Temple with his staff, and his shoes, with his purse, and dust upon his feet: and that none make it his common thoroughfare, nor make it a place of spitting."[11]

Jesus was also fulfilling a messianic prophecy about cleansing the temple. A large body of scriptural material had been accumulated by the scribes that defined the coming Messiah and His activity. Some was false—for instance, the idea that the Messiah could not be hurt (angels would bear Him up lest He dash His foot against a stone). Others were consistent with the intent of God and His mission for the Messiah. Cleaning the temple was one of those consistent evidences of the true Messiah.

SESSION 6. WHEN REAL LOVE LEADS TO BIG TROUBLE

The point Jesus is making in Mark 13:1-13 is, "Don't _____. I'm still in control."

Eschatology is about the doctrine of _____ _____—the return of Christ.

Jesus didn't just _____ us. He took our _____.

The highlight of Jesus' lesson on the fig tree is that there will be no more _____ and _____ when He returns.

In Mark 13:32 Jesus said that even He _____ _____ _____ when He will return.

Satan knows his time is _____.

Video sessions available for purchase at
www.lifeway.com/GospelofMark

Discussion Questions:

How often do you worry about the future or end times?

What peace and assurance do you know and experience because of your relationship with Jesus?

In the time that each of us is given, how can we share Jesus with others and help them understand the truth of the gospel?

THE BEAUTIFUL OUTCOME OF OUR LORD'S BETRAYAL

REAL LIFE

"The lash on his back, the thorns on his head, the spit on his cheek, the bruises on his face, the nails in his hands, the spear in his side, the scorn of the rulers, the betrayal of his friend, the desertion by his disciples—these were all the result of sin, and all designed by God to destroy the power of sin."[1]
JOHN PIPER

When I was in middle school I went to a youth rally in Orlando where I heard a pastor tell a story that haunted me for a long time. It went something like this:

Once upon a time there was a very kind man who lived in quaint log cabin in a remote area of the Great White North with his lovely wife and beloved son, who'd been born to them after over a decade of infertility. The man made an honest living operating a drawbridge that allowed twice daily commuter trains to pass safely over a large lake in the mountains where they lived.

The drawbridge operator's little boy was both his namesake and the apple of his eye, so it delighted him when Junior accompanied him to work every Saturday. He often let him sit on his lap and push the button to lower the drawbridge and then wave cheerfully at the train passengers whizzing passed the control booth on their way to the big city. But one Saturday Junior brought a bright red ball to entertain himself with and moments before the afternoon train rolled through, the ball rolled away from him down the hill and came to rest on the tracks below.

The train's whistle drowned out the father's bellowed warning not to chase after the ball, but he saw the train barrel around the bend at the exact moment he saw his boy take off toward the ball. He had a split second to choose whether to leave the control booth and rescue his child, thereby condemning hundreds of commuters to their death because he'd have to forgo lowering the drawbridge to do so, or he could sit tight in the booth and do his job, thereby saving hundreds of strangers yet crushing his only son in the process.

He instinctively chose the latter. And then sat in stunned horror while hundreds of oblivious men, women, and children he'd probably never even meet hurtled past with hands raised in happy greeting.

When the youth pastor got to the end of the story he added soberly, "And that's exactly what God did for every single one of us. He crushed Jesus, His only begotten Son, to rescue you." Of course, there was a huge altar call response that night as tons of kids—including myself—tearfully raced to the front of the National Guard Armory/youth revival site burdened with fresh guilt over the fact that because of our reprehensible behavior, God panicked and hit some dreadful button in heaven that condemned dear Jesus to death on a cross. Most of my girlfriends and I wept bitterly all the way home in an old fifteen-passenger church van, while the boys stared mournfully out the window at flickering Interstate billboards because this was an era before hand-held high-tech devices, not long after all the dinosaurs died.

For years afterwards I wondered and worried about that drawbridge operator and his wife. I thought about how hard Christmas morning must be with their son's limp stocking hanging over the fireplace. How bleak his birthday must now be for them. How that father must be in continual torment over whether he did the right thing. How that mother must've eventually walked away from the cabin, the lake, the menacing drawbridge, and their once-strong marriage because surely she was unable to cope with the constant reminders of her grief.

It wasn't until decades later, during a seminary class on sound biblical teaching principles, that I found out the train story was a complete fabrication. It never actually happened. It's the spiritual edition of an urban legend and was conjured up by some creative, albeit manipulative, soul as an illustrative "tool" to help people recognize the magnitude of their sin.

Calvary was not the panicked result of God choosing to kill Jesus so as to rescue mankind. It was not a last-minute decision. It was not some gut-wrenching version of *Sophie's Choice*. There is no anguished operator in a divine drawbridge booth. Instead the Creator of the universe planned every detail of His Son's betrayal, the trumped up charges, the bogus trial, Pilate's political side step, and the laborious *Via Doloroso*. God chose the nails that would be driven into His boy's wrists and feet. He grew the trees that would sprout the thorns that would be woven into a mock crown and cruelly jammed onto His precious only Child's head.

Our Savior's murder was not a knee-jerk reaction. It was a carefully and divinely orchestrated mission of mercy.

READ ACTS 2:22-23. How would you paraphrase these verses so that a child could understand them? What term would you use in place of "delivered up"?

READ MARK 8:31-33 AND ACTS 4:23-28. How would you describe the change that took place in Peter regarding the crucifixion of Christ over the course of about three months—the approximate amount of time between these two passages?

READ ISAIAH 53:10. How does this one verse disprove the drawbridge-operator illustration?

REAL TRUTH

When I was in the fifth grade I was singled out by the school bully—a very large girl named Bullia (not her real name of course because we've lost touch and I'm afraid she might still have anger management issues), who was a few years older than the rest of our class and exploited her superior height, weight, and age to dispense intimidating dirty looks, give ear-ringing hallway head-thumps, and slug anyone who crossed her. We'd been classmates since the second grade and I'd never had a problem with Bullia until the boys asked me to join in their playground soccer match instead of her one day at recess. At which she glowered and, when our P.E. teacher was out of earshot, menacingly announced she was going to beat me up as soon as she got the chance.

If I close my eyes and focus, I can almost hear the apprehensive murmurings that rumbled across the playground afterwards like a tidal wave of whispers, followed by the exhalation of twenty-five ten-year-olds who were just thankful it was me and not them.

Once we all filed back into Mr. Garrett's classroom and sat down, my best friend Timidity (also not her real name but she's long since apologized for what happens next so she'll remain anonymous) passed me a note suggesting we get a bathroom pass so as to strategize about how to respond to Bullia's threat. Why we didn't anticipate that Bullia would request a bathroom pass immediately after us and barge into our secret meeting is a mystery. I can still picture how her shoulders were almost as wide as the entrance and how her brown eyes narrowed into small aggressive slits when she set her focus on me with the obvious intent of pummeling me into oblivion. I also remember the look of pure terror that flashed across Timidity's face and the blur of her yellow shirt as she whirled away from me, rushed into a stall, and locked the door behind her, leaving me alone to face our elementary school Goliath.

Betrayal. My guess is you've got a few stories of your own that involve being stranded. Thrown under the bus. Left hanging.

> What's the earliest memory you have of betrayal—like maybe a sibling letting you take the fall for something they actually did that incurred the wrath of your mom or dad?

Not only did God compose the sober symphony of Calvary, He arranged the disharmonic notes of betrayal leading up to His Son's death:

> They came to an area called Gethsemane. Jesus told his disciples, "Sit here while I pray." He took Peter, James, and John with him. He plunged into a sinkhole of dreadful agony. He told them, "I feel bad enough right now to die. Stay here and keep vigil with me." Going a little ahead, he fell to the ground and prayed for a way out: "Papa, Father, you can—can't you?—get me out of this. Take this cup away from me. But please, not what I want—what do *you* want?"
>
> He came back and found them sound asleep. He said to Peter, "Simon, you went to sleep on me? Can't you stick it out with me a single hour? Stay alert, be in prayer, so you don't enter the danger zone without even knowing it. Don't be naive. Part of you is eager, ready for anything in God; but another part is as lazy as an old dog sleeping by the fire."
>
> He then went back and prayed the same prayer. Returning, he again found them sound asleep. They simply couldn't keep their eyes open, and they didn't have a plausible excuse.
>
> He came back a third time and said, "Are you going to sleep all night? No—you've slept long enough. Time's up. The Son of Man is about to be betrayed into the hands of sinners. Get up. Let's get going. My betrayer has arrived."
>
> No sooner were the words out of his mouth when Judas, the one out of the Twelve, showed up, and with him a gang of ruffians, sent by the high priests, religion scholars, and leaders, brandishing swords and clubs. The betrayer had worked out a signal with them: "The one I kiss, that's the one—seize him. Make sure he doesn't get away." He went straight to Jesus and said, "Rabbi!" and kissed him. The others then grabbed him and roughed him up. One of the men standing there unsheathed his sword, swung, and came down on the Chief Priest's servant, lopping off the man's ear.
> MARK 14:32-43, THE MESSAGE

A few nights ago, several of us had gathered to have dinner at my pastor's house, and because most of us around the table are big talkers and loud laughers, we ended up having an uproariously good time sharing our most embarrassing moments. We all had some pretty cringe-worthy train wrecks to entertain our fellow diners with, but my dear friend Scott Hamilton—who's best known for being an Olympic gold medalist but his true claim to fame is marrying one of the kindest, most compassionate women in the entire world, Tracie—took home the top prize.

He began his story with the dry statement, "OK, first of all I'm a short, bald man who used to wear leotards, so there's that!" Then he went on to paint the scene at a sold-out ice show that took place in a huge arena not long after he'd won the Olympic gold medal in men's figure skating at Sarajevo in 1984. Of course he was the star of the show so his introduction rivaled that of a king; huge spotlights were illuminated, fog rolled across the floor of the rink, the music swelled to a crescendo, and then Scott came gliding into the light holding a dramatic pose and wearing a skin tight Superman costume complete with billowing cape. He said the roar of the crowd was so loud it practically held him up during the first triple jump in his program, so he couldn't help thinking, "Man, I am so on tonight!"

However, that packed to capacity, cheering-their-guts-out audience also generated a lot of heat. Which caused a thin layer of water to form on top of the ice, which threw the reigning men's world figure skating champion just a hair off balance as he launched into his next gravity-defying leap, which caused him to catch both toe picks on the landing. And because toe picks stuck in ice act like a hinge, Scott then belly-flopped unceremoniously to the ice with the resounding wet smack of a hooked fish being slapped on the bow of a bass boat just prior to being filleted by some happy angler! Adding insult to injury, when he gamely hopped up to finish the rest of the routine, he looked down to see the watery crash had left a large, very noticeable circular stain on his pants which left him looking less like Superman and more like a little boy who'd just had an accident!

By the end of Scott's hilariously re-enacted, self-effacing story, we were all laughing so hard we were in danger of having accidents as well. But then the conversation took a more serious turn, and we talked about how a hero who stumbles is so much more approachable than one who appears infallible. Now please, please hear me when I say I. Do. Not. Believe. King. Jesus. Is. Anything. Less. Than. Perfect. Our Creator Redeemer is not fallible. However, what happened when He approached the garden of Gethsemane for the last time definitely makes Him more approachable.

He "plunged into a sinkhole of dreadful agony" and then "fell to the ground and prayed for a way out" (The Message).

In Tim Keller's book *Jesus the King*, he asks (and ultimately answers) the question that surely many wonder but rarely articulate with regards to what happened in the garden of Gethsemane: *Why is it that many of Jesus' followers have died "better" than Jesus?*[2] Because unlike the two female martyrs from our first video session, Perpetua and Felicitas, and thousands of others like them who stoically endured unspeakable horrors which led to their physical death for the sake of the gospel, Jesus did not square His holy shoulders and face the cross with a stiff upper lip initially. He agonized over His pending sacrificial death.

REREAD HEBREWS 4:14-15 AND 1 PETER 2:19-25. How does the fact that we have an empathetic Hero help you emulate Him when you're being unfairly persecuted or subject to a humiliating situation?

READ HEBREWS 12:2. What insight does this verse give regarding Jesus' submission to the crucifixion despite the fact that meant He'd assume the culpability and shame accrued by every past and future evil of mankind thereby forfeiting communion with God?

According to Dr. Keller, the reality of what He was about to lose caused our Lord to stagger: God is the Source of all love, all life, and all coherence. Therefore exclusion from God is exclusion from the Source of all light, all love, and all coherence. Jesus began to experience the spiritual, cosmic, infinite disintegration that would happen when He became separated from His Father on the cross. Jesus began to experience merely a foretaste of that, and He staggered.[3]

Yet instead of catching Jesus before He hit the pavement, like even an acquaintance would be compelled to, His three closest friends were catching a few Zs. Rather than having His back, Peter, James, and John were having a snooze. And it goes from bad to worse because while those three were still rubbing the sleep from their eyes and sheepishly smoothing down slumber-mussed hair, another disciple sells Him out with the cruelest kiss in history:

> At once, while Jesus was still speaking, Judas, one of the twelve apostles, came up. With him were many people carrying swords and clubs who had been sent from the leading priests, the teachers of the law, and the Jewish elders. Judas had planned a signal for them, saying, "The man I kiss is Jesus. Arrest him and guard him while you lead him away." So Judas went straight to Jesus and said, "Teacher!" and kissed him. Then the people grabbed Jesus and arrested him. One of his followers standing nearby pulled out his sword and struck the servant of the high priest and cut off his ear. Then Jesus said, "You came to get me with swords and clubs as if I were a criminal. Every day I was with you teaching in the Temple, and you did not arrest me there. But all these things have happened to make the Scriptures come true."
> MARK 14:43-49, NCV

Even though Jesus knew Judas was going to exchange his devotion for silver (John 13:21), I wonder if He winced when His former friend leaned forward with pursed lips that night. I also wonder if His incarnate shoulders sagged when the rest of that "band of brothers" turned tail and ran after dirty cops jerked His arms behind His back and slapped cuffs on our Savior:

Then all of Jesus' followers left him and ran away.
MARK 14:50, NCV

When the going got tough, almost everybody bailed on the Messiah. Instead of exhibiting character, His followers resembled a cast of cartoon weaklings who cowered in fear when religious bullies kicked sand on the Son of God.

> **READ MARK 14:51-52.** In the first video session we talked about how the consensus of biblical scholarship agrees that it was likely Mark who "ran away naked." Now that we're nearing the end of his Gospel account, how do you think that humiliating early episode in his life affected the way he told the story of Jesus?

> If you somehow discovered that you were going to suffer a violent, disgraceful death in the next day or two, how do you think you'd respond?

> If you had to distill the concept of character/integrity into a few words what would they be?

My friend Buster—a silver-haired hero of a man with a Golden Gloves national boxing championship, a Silver Star from the Korean War, a slew of patents, and decades at the helm of international corporations under his belt—and I had a long conversation about what character looks like the other day. He said one of the most effective character-building seasons of his life was his plebe year at West Point almost fifty years ago. He explained as newbies on that historic military campus they were allowed only three responses to whatever question older classmen posed. The trio of permissible replies were: "No Sir." "Yes Sir." "No excuse, Sir." Then he added sagely, "Lisa, when you don't have the option of making excuses, you learn not to."

I love gleaning life lessons from Buster, so I asked him if he had any other advice on the subject. After pausing to reflect for a few seconds, he replied thoughtfully, "Have courage and be kind." I said, "Did you learn that at West Point too?" His blue eyes twinkled, and there was laughter in his voice when he replied, "Nope, that's from the new Cinderella movie. I've watched it three times with my granddaughters!"

READ MARK 14:53–15:15. How many more betrayals—by both friends and enemies—can you count from the garden of Gethsemane to the interior of the governor's palace?

READ JOHN 21 AND MATTHEW 16:18. Peter infamously betrayed Jesus three times—vehemently and vulgarly—yet Jesus not only forgave him, He prophesied that Peter was the "rock" He was going to build the New Testament church upon. How would you describe the difference between simply pardoning someone or pardoning someone and then entrusting them to be an integral part of your life and mission?

Do you have any close teammates who were formerly rivals? If so, how did the transition from foe to friend happen?

REAL ACHE

From hearing the sounds of His dear friends' snores in between His own ragged sobs of grief in Gethsemane to observing the pathetic charade of Pilate's hand washing, Jesus endured a continuum of unjustified infidelity throughout the last few days of His earthly life that would test the character of any man. But of course, He wasn't just any man. He is the Christ—the Anointed One our Heavenly Father commissioned and purposed to receive the punishment we deserve. Which means He wasn't called to simply stand firm in the face of hardship like some skinny but determined freshman at a military school— He was called to bend toward betrayal. To lean into the vicious lies being spewed about Him. To humbly accept a completely undeserved capital punishment charge without any kind of appeal. To mute His own omnipotent roar and become the Passover Lamb:

> And the soldiers led him away inside the palace (that is, the governor's headquarters), and they called together the whole battalion. And they clothed him in a purple cloak, and twisting together a crown of thorns, they put it on him. And they began to salute him, "Hail, King of the Jews!" And they were striking his head with a reed and spitting on him and kneeling down in homage to him. And when they had mocked him, they stripped him of the purple cloak and put his own clothes on him. And they led him out to crucify him.
> MARK 15:16-20

A few years ago, my friend Cheryl—who's the women's ministry director at a large church in Texas—told me she was walking down a church hallway on a weekday when she heard sobs coming from the library. She turned and hurried toward the cries, thinking someone was obviously distraught and needed help. She was surprised to discover that the weeping was coming from one of their missionaries, who was home on furlough for a few months. He and his wife had dedicated their lives to sharing the living hope of Jesus and translating the Bible into the language of a small, largely unreached people group who live in a remote area in West Africa. When she approached him and gently asked if he was OK he responded, "Oh, I'll be OK, Cheryl. It's just that I'm translating the crucifixion."

We should all be so moved by what happened on that very first "Good" Friday.

Jeering Roman soldiers jammed a wreath of thorns on Jesus' head to mock His claim of being King. They wrapped His bruised and bleeding body in a violet robe symbolizing royalty to ridicule Him. They punched Him and spit on Him. Furthermore, all of this took place after Jesus had been scourged, which meant He'd already been tied to a post and beaten with a leather whip that was interwoven with pieces of bone and metal that tore through His skin, probably exposing muscle and bone.

The Lion of Judah could've let out a roar and ripped His assailants to pieces if He had wanted. Instead, He humbly remained the Passover Lamb and stumbled up a hill to His own slaughter. The King of all kings allowed mean-spirited strangers to pound nails into His wrists and feet and hoist Him up on a cross between two common criminals. He condescended to a horrific and humiliating death:

> And it was the third hour when they crucified him. And the inscription of the charge against him read, "The King of the Jews." And with him they crucified two robbers, one on his right and one on his left. And those who passed by derided him, wagging their heads and saying, "Aha! You who would destroy the temple and rebuild it in three days, save yourself, and come down from the cross!" So also the chief priests with the scribes mocked him to one another, saying, "He saved others; he cannot save himself. Let the Christ, the King of Israel, come down now from the cross that we may see and believe." Those who were crucified with him also reviled him.
> MARK 15:25-32

> Less than a week before, Jesus was being hailed as a hero when He entered Jerusalem; now He's being crucified before a taunting, bloodthirsty mob. What do you think His followers were feeling as they observed this shocking reversal from adulation to degradation?

READ PSALM 22. What lyrics provoke the most sorrow in you? What specific aspect of the crucifixion makes you the most uncomfortable? Explain why.

Last month I had a speaking engagement in California and my thoughtful friend Pam—who's a Disneyland® VIP—invited me to come out early and bring Missy so that she could treat us to a special day at the park. We had so much fun swaying on the swinging gondola, riding in the simulated Star Wars battleship, racing on the Cars track, and careening up and down Thunder Mountain. I grew up twenty miles north of Orlando, Florida, so I'd reached the stage of not caring if I ever went to another theme park again decades ago. But being at Disneyland with my wide-eyed, giggling six-year-old daughter was totally and wonderfully different than the tantrum-throwing-children-and-teeming-masses-of-grumpy-adults traumas of my past. Plus, because of Pam's generosity, we had Fast Passes and didn't have to wait in the long lines! The only downside was that it was an atypical, record-breaking 100+ degree October day in California, which is the only excuse I have for my foolish lapse in judgment toward the end of our Disneyland experience.

I'm one of those yahoo parents who blithely held hands with her six-year-old daughter and walked-without-really-seeing into the dark, cavernous venue of Space Mountain. I'm one of those yahoo parents who mindlessly chatted while walking down the ramp to the loading zone thereby blocking out the screams of current Space Mountain participants and not cluing into the fact that Space Mountain is not appropriate for her SIX-YEAR-OLD DAUGHTER WHO'S ADOPTED FROM HAITI WHERE THEY DON'T HAVE THEME PARKS, MUCH LESS UBER SCARY ROLLER COASTERS. It wasn't until Missy and I were sitting side-by-side in the steel coaster car with the bar lowered securely over our laps and lurching forward that I thought, *Yikes, she is way too young to be on this rrrriii-iddddeeee* … Of course by then it was too late because we were hurtling through the black abyss before I'd finished the thought.

To say I held on to Missy for dear life is putting it mildly. I'm surprised her beautiful brown right bicep and the inner thigh of her darling left leg don't have my fingerprints permanently embedded. Now because I wasn't holding on to my bar, I bounced around like a pin-ball and things shot out of my pockets like fizz from a shaken coke can. However, I was pretty sure that even without hanging on my fluffy thighs would prevent me from being launched and I was determined to keep my child from becoming flying debris, so I held on to her as tightly as I could and whispered, "I'm right here, baby. It's going to be OK. This ride is going to be over in just a minute" over and over again. Because the interior of that crazy coaster is deafeningly loud and pitch black dark, I didn't know if she could hear me and I couldn't see her expression, so I could only hope she wasn't crying and pray she wouldn't be psychologically scarred for life.

When we finally lurched back into the light at the end of the ride, I was very relieved to see that she wasn't crying and was sitting up ramrod straight with a serious expression on her face. I blurted out, "Honey, I'm so sorry… are you OK?" To which she replied with comical authority, "Yes ma'am. But I do NOT like dat Space Moun Tan. It is too dawk and too scarwee."

Dark and scary would be an apt description for what happened from the sixth hour until the ninth hour that Jesus hung on the old rugged cross:

> And when the sixth hour had come, there was darkness over the whole land until the ninth hour. And at the ninth hour Jesus cried with a loud voice, "Eloi, Eloi, lema sabachthani?" which means, "My God, my God, why have you forsaken me?" And some of the bystanders hearing it said, "Behold, he is calling Elijah." And someone ran and filled a sponge with sour wine, put it on a reed and gave it to him to drink, saying, "Wait, let us see whether Elijah will come to take him down." And Jesus uttered a loud cry and breathed his last. And the curtain of the temple was torn in two, from top to bottom.
> MARK 15:33-38

From noon until 3 P.M. on the day the curse of inevitable doom was lifted from humanity, Jerusalem was plunged into complete and eerie darkness. If ache could be illustrated by a weather forecast, it would be like that ancient Friday afternoon when the Holy City was totally devoid of light causing it to be a very dawk and very scarwee place.

READ ISAIAH 13:9-10 AND JEREMIAH 15:6-9. What do these passages suggest about supernatural darkness (e.g., sunlessness that doesn't coincide with nighttime)?

READ EXODUS 10:21-23. How does the plague of darkness preceding Passover compare to the darkness of Calvary?

If someone asked you, "Why did Jesus have to die?" how would you answer that person?

REAL HOPE

I've gotten parenting credit I don't deserve (some of you are probably nodding your heads after my Space Mountain confession) for the fact that Missy and I have had an uncommonly smooth adoption transition. And while I'd like to think she connected with me so quickly because I'm such a good mama, the truth is our relatively fast and deep mother-daughter bond is Fifi's fruit. Fifi is Missy's great aunt. She's the sickly, gentle, huge-hearted saint who took my little girl in when her lovely biological mama was too sick from a disease called AIDS (which she never knew she had because like far too many impoverished people barely surviving in Third World countries, Marie had never been diagnosed) to care for her. Too weak to produce milk, much less scrounge for food for her infant. Too cold to snuggle her daughter at night and provide necessary warmth. So Fifi stepped in to rescue Missy and is the main reason my baby girl survived infancy. Fifi is also the one who championed me to be her new mama. In spite of the fact that I was an American stranger who, if approved to adopt her beloved great niece, would take her to a land far, far away called Tennessee filled with four-wheel drive trucks and fried food.

The first time I met Fifi she smiled shyly and then placed this scowling toddler named Missy into my arms and said to her firmly in Creole, "This is your white mama." Both of us protested; I wanted to give Missy ample time to warm up to me, and Missy was obviously alarmed by my pale ampleness. But Fifi just smiled again shyly and crossed her arms, quietly refusing to take the indignant two-and-a-half year old back into her embrace. It took a few minutes but when my then very wary baby girl realized she didn't have a choice, she grudgingly relented to let me feed her beans and rice and bounce her on my hip. The next day, at Fifi's insistence, Missy allowed me to hold her hand and walk around the village for an hour. The second night I was there, Missy condescended to sit on my lap during a stifling hot worship service, after Fifi gave her a very direct you'd-better-mind-me-right-now-young-lady look. With each new baby-step milestone in our budding relationship, Fifi's smile got wider and she'd nod with approval. When I hugged her fiercely before leaving at the end of that first of many visits, all the while babbling about how grateful I was, she replied simply, "I love you. Praise Jesus," which was one of the only English phrases she knew.

Over the next two years those five words became our regular conversation. During long, hot bumpy bus rides together from their village to Port au Prince for a doctor's check-up or an appointment with the U.S. Embassy, Fifi would hold my hand the entire two to three hour trip and repeat softly, "I love you. Praise Jesus" every thirty minutes or so. When I tried to engage her with my pitiable attempts to speak Creole (I still have several intro to Creole books in my library and an "easy" English-Creole app on my phone, but much like Frenchy in *Grease*, I proved to be a language school drop-out), she'd nod and listen patiently but would inevitably respond with, "I love you. Praise Jesus."

Finally, on April 14, 2014, when I hugged Fifi with tears streaming down my face, Missy sleeping in my arms, and clutching a manila folder with Haitian and American documents stating that I was now legally Missy's mama, she squeezed both of my hands, looked deep into my eyes and said again, "I love you. Praise Jesus." By then I knew what she really meant by those five words was, "I'm entrusting you to take good care of her. It's breaking my heart to know I'll probably only see her again a few times before I die, but I know this is what's best for her. Remember that she likes her mangoes on the firm side and she loves to be sung to sleep. Don't let her be lazy in school, or be disrespectful, or eat with her mouth open, or bite her fingernails, or forget how very much I loved her. OK, I'm going to kiss her head one last time and try to memorize her face and her precious little girl smell and the shape of her toes before I turn my head. And please know the reason I won't watch y'all drive away toward the airport isn't because I'm ambivalent—it's so I won't chase the van and beg you not to leave quite yet."

Fifi willingly gave up her claim on my daughter's heart so that my daughter could live. Hers is one of the most sacrificial affections I've ever had the privilege of witnessing. How much more so is our Heavenly Father's affection for us? He willingly watched His only begotten Son depart from Glory knowing that He would be pierced for our transgressions. With the full knowledge that Jesus would soon scream in agony, "Dad, Dad, why have You forsaken Me?" God also knew He wasn't going to be able to lift a finger to help His incarnate child when He cried out from that cursed tree. Because in order for His image-bearers to live, His boy had to die.

I know it's incredibly anthropomorphic to ascribe human emotion to God the Father, but the mama in me hopes that when He heard the curtain rip He grinned:

> And Jesus uttered a loud cry and breathed his last. And the
> curtain of the temple was torn in two, from top to bottom.
> MARK 15:37-38

Don't forget that massive curtain—which ancient rabbinic sources say was several thousand pounds and took 300 people to move—was torn in two, thereby removing the separation and allowing us access to God's mercy. I also love that Mark clarifies that the curtain was ripped "from top to bottom" (v.38), implying that God Himself ripped that fancy fabric!

Plus, it was "torn in two, from top to bottom" at the ninth hour, which meant this massive 60 foot long and 30 foot wide curtain ripped in half causing an enormous crash at three o'clock in the afternoon, right about the time the temple priests were standing directly in front of it dutifully going through the motions of religion. To say those poor guys were a little startled is like saying a bear is a little hungry when it wakes up from hibernation!

READ ACTS 6:7. Do you think the revival that swept through the priesthood had anything to do the whole veil-tearing drama?

READ EXODUS 30:10 AND HEBREWS 9:1-9. What's the symbolic significance of the temple curtain being torn?

When has there been a figurative veil-tearing moment in your spiritual life when you felt like a barrier between you and God was removed?

Then when the centurion—who'd just observed the crucifixion—exclaimed with concise enthusiasm:

"Truly this man was the Son of God!"
MARK 15:39B

I like to picture God chuckling and saying to Himself, "Yep, He sure is!" Finally three days later, when Jesus' resurrection verified His divine DNA (Mark 16; John 20:1-18), and the Lion came roaring back to life holding the keys of hell and death He'd just ripped from Satan's grimy hand—well, then I imagine the Alpha and Omega taking a victory lap around heaven before beginning to plan His Son's welcome home party!

When you really ponder the symbol of a cross, do you feel more sorrowful or hopeful?

What's the "Oh wow, surely Jesus is the Son of God" moment in your life?

ROMAN CRUCIFIXION

Crucifixion was not a Roman invention. It was introduced to the west from the eastern cultures where Assyrians, Phoenicians, and Persians practiced it for a thousand years before Christ. Alexander the Great introduced the practice to Egypt and Carthage, and the Romans probably learned it in the first century BC from the Carthaginians.

Initially, the Romans used crucifixion not as a method of execution but as an official punishment for slaves found guilty of transgressions. During this period, the slave was required to proclaim his offense while marching through the neighborhood with a wooden beam placed across his neck and bound to his arms. Later, the humiliation and punishment was increased by adding the practice of stripping and scourging the victim. By the first century AD, crucifixion had developed into a method of execution for certain crimes. In Palestine, those crimes usually were robbery, tumult, and sedition against Rome.[4]

Crucifixion later was used to punish foreign captives, rebels, and fugitives, particularly during times of war and revolt. Captured enemies and rebels often were crucified in masses. In 71 BC the Roman army suppressed a revolt in Spartacus by lining the road from Capua to Rome with 6,000 rebels hanging on crosses. After the rebellion in Judea in AD 7, the Romans crucified 2,000 Jews in Jerusalem. During Titus' siege of Jerusalem in AD 70, soldiers crucified as many as 500 Jews a day for several months.[5]

There is some difference of opinion whether the Jews in Palestine possessed legal authority to impose the death sentence. John 18:31 apparently denies that the Jewish leaders had the legal privilege to exercise capital punishment. They asked Pilate to impose the sentence on Jesus because "it was not lawful for us to put any man to death." The Jews probably had lost this legal privilege when their land became a Roman province in AD 6. Josephus wrote of the first Roman procurator in Palestine, Coponius, as having the "power of life and death put into his hands by Caesar" (*Wars* 2/8/1), the same powers Pilate claimed for himself in John 19:10. Josephus nowhere mentioned any such Jewish authority in this period.

Some scholars insist the Romans, until AD 70, permitted Jewish leaders to exercise the death penalty against Jews alone and only in regard to religious matters. They cite the Temple inscription in Greek, warning Gentiles not to proceed beyond their court under pain of death.[6] If this argument was true, the Jews probably could have stoned Jesus for blasphemy. Failing to establish their case, however, they fabricated the political charge of sedition, which was in Pilate's province. The Greek word used in John 18:31 for "put to death" is *apokteino*, which implies bloodshed. In crucifixion bloodshed was certain but not in stoning. The Jews, being scrupulous about purity at Passover, knew

Adapted from "Roman Crucifixion" by Gary K. Halbrook, *Biblical Illustrator*, Winter 1990, 3, 7-10.

that shedding blood at this season would render them lawfully unclean.

The stoning of Stephen (Acts 7) and the persecution of the Christians by Saul (Acts 9:1) suggest one of two things: either (1) the Jews possessed the capital penalty in religious matters for Jews who were not Roman citizens or (2) considerable laxity on the part of Rome prevailed at times.[7]

During times of war and rebellion, little attention was paid to the way in which crucifixions were done. In peacetime, however, persons authorized by the Roman courts to perform crucifixions followed definite rules. Specific locations were designated for crucifixions; in Jerusalem it was Golgotha.[8]

After the sentence of crucifixion was delivered, the execution was supervised by an official known as the *Carnifix Serarum*. The unfortunate victim was taken from the tribunal hall, stripped, bound to a column, and scourged either with a stick or *flagellum*. Following the beating, the horizontal beam was placed on the victim's shoulders and he was forced to begin the long, humiliating march to the execution site. The *titulus*, a sign announcing the condemned man's crime, either was carried in front by a soldier or attached to the beam. At the execution site, the victim was attached to the horizontal beam by ropes or nails (through the wrists) and then the cross beam was hoisted up the vertical stake. The crucifixion process damaged no vital part of the body.[9]

The method of crucifixion appears to have been limited only by materials available and the imagination of the Roman executioners. In time they developed means to extend the agony of the condemned. For instance, while hanging from the crossbar, the sufferer found breathing difficult. At first, he was able to pull himself up to breathe for perhaps a minute at a time. As he became weaker, movement became increasingly difficult and finally impossible. Death came from the muscular spasms and asphyxia usually within two to three hours.[10]

Normally, the Romans left the crucified victim to die slowly of sheer physical exhaustion leading to suffocation. Whenever a crucifixion occurred on a day prior to a Jewish holy day (Passover in the case of Jesus), Roman law relented to Jewish tradition that required burial on the day of execution. For this reason, the executioners broke the legs of the crucified so they could not lift themselves to breathe, thus hastening death by trauma. This permitted burial before nightfall, when the holy day began.

Roman crucifixion ranks among the most heartless and inhuman forms of torture and death yet contrived. That such a cruel practice could be transformed into a means of salvation testifies powerfully to God's grace and mercy for all the world.

SESSION 7. SAVING THE LAST FOR BEST

Reflect on 1 Corinthians 1:26-31:

> For consider your calling, brothers: not many of you were wise
> according to worldly standards, not many were powerful, not many
> were of noble birth. But God chose what is foolish in the world to
> shame the wise; God chose what is weak in the world to shame
> the strong; God chose what is low and despised in the world, even
> things that are not, to bring to nothing things that are, so that no
> human being might boast in the presence of God. And because
> of him you are in Christ Jesus, who became to us wisdom from
> God, righteousness and sanctification and redemption, so that,
> as it is written, "Let the one who boasts, boast in the Lord."
> 1 CORINTHIANS 1:26-3

How will you proclaim that you love the Lord Jesus with all your heart to
the aching world around you?

Discussion Questions:

Do you think Jesus is better off with you as one of His followers?

What are examples of the seasons in your life when you felt you were "less than" and how did the Lord help you to get out of those seasons?

How have you "seen" the Lord and His work in your life and in the lives of others?

How will you proclaim the hope of the gospel to those around you after this Bible study?

ENDNOTES

WEEK ONE:

1. C.S. Lewis, *Surprised by Joy: The Shape of My Early Life* (Orlando: Harcourt Inc., 1955), 228-229.

2. *Webster's Encyclopedic Unabridged Dictionary of the English Language*, "Synoptic" (San Diego: Thunder Bay Press, 2001), 1929.

3. James A. Brooks, *The New American Commentary: Mark* (Nashville: B&H Publishing Group, 1991), 19-25.

4. Daniel L. Akin, *Christ-Centered Exposition Commentary: Exalting Jesus in Mark* (Nashville: B&H Publishing Group, 2014), 40.

5. Encyclopædia Britannica Online, s. v. "Hebrew Bible", accessed January 13, 2016, *http://www. britannica.com/topic/Hebrew-Bible*.

6. Akin, *Christ-Centered Exposition Commentary: Exalting Jesus in Mark*, 26-27.

7. Anne Lamott, *Plan B: Further Thoughts on Faith* (New York: Riverhead Books, 2005), 54-55.

8. The Tim Keller's quote is from his 2006 sermon series on Mark called "King's Cross: The Gospel of Mark" and the particular sermon title it came from was "Jesus On the Mount, Jesus Off the Mount." I downloaded the sermon series from the Redeemer Presbyterian Church (where he pastors in New York) resource website: *GospelinLife.com*.

9. Concerning Mark, Papias also said, "he was in company with Peter, who gave him such instruction as was necessary … wherefore Mark has not erred in any thing, by writing some things as he recorded them; for he was carefully attentive to one thing, not to pass by any thing that he heard, or to state any thing falsely in these accounts." *Eusebius' Ecclesiastical History: Complete and Unabridged*, trans. C.F. Cruse (Peabody, MA: Hendrickson Publishers, 1998), 3.39.15 (pp. 105-106).

10. D.A. Carson, Douglas J. Moo, and Leon Morris, *An Introduction to the New Testament* (Grand Rapids: Zondervan, 1992), 97-98.

WEEK TWO:

1. Akin, *Christ-Centered Exposition*, 95.

2. James Strong, *Strong's Greek Hebrew Dictionary* (Nashville: Thomas Nelson, 2009), s.v. "akouo."

3. Robert James Dr. Utley, *The Gospel According to Peter: Mark and I & II Peter*, vol. 2, *Study Guide Commentary Series* (Marshall, Texas: Bible Lessons International, 2000), 54.

4. Gerhard Kittel, Geoffrey W. Bromiley, and Gerhard Friedrich, eds., *Theological Dictionary of the New Testament* (Grand Rapids, MI: Eerdmans, 1964–), 216.

5. C.H. Dodd, *The Parables of the Kingdom* (London: Charles Scribner's Sons, 1961), 21.

6. Charles H. Spurgeon, Sermon #2004, "The Lover of God's Law Filled with Peace," delivered on January 22, 1888, Metropolitan Tabernacle, Newington, http://www.spurgeongems.org/vols34-36/chs2004.pdf

7. William L. Lane, *The New International Commentary on the New Testament: The Gospel of Mark* (Grand Rapids: William B. Eerdmans Publishing, 1974), 151.

8. From the *New Revised Standard Version of the Bible* copyright © 1989 by the Division of Christian Education of the National Council of Churches of Christ in the United States of America. Used by permission. All rights reserved.

9. F.S. Frick, "Ecology, Agriculture and Patters of Settlement," in *The Words of Ancient Israel,* ed. R.E. Clements (Cambridge: Cambridge University Press, 1989), 71-77.

10. D.H.K. Amiran, "Land Use in Israel," in *Land Use in Semi-Arid Mediterranean Climates* (Paris: UNESCO, 1964), 104.

11. Ibid., 110-111.

12. Charles F. Pfeiffer, *The Biblical World* (Grand Rapids: Baker Book House, 1966) 22, 24.

13. Frick, 77-78.

14. Ibid., 78.

WEEK THREE:

1. *Webster's Encyclopedic Unabridged Dictionary of the English Language*, "scandal" (San Diego, CA; Thunder Bay Press, 2001), 1710.

2. Akin, *Christ-Centered Exposition*, 122.

3. Ibid., 139.

4. James Strong, *Strong's Greek Hebrew Dictionary* (Nashville: Thomas Nelson, 2009), s.v. "kynarion."

5. Tim Keller, *King's Cross: The Story of the World in the Life of Jesus* (New York: Dutton of Penguin Group, 2011), 86.

6. Akin, *Christ-Centered Exposition*, 156.

7. From the hymn by Lidie H. Edmunds, "My Faith Has Found a Resting Place."

8. Although this article does not treat Jesus' exorcism ministry, five of Jesus' exorcisms resulted in physical healing. The article does not include instances of Jesus raising persons from the dead.

9. Matt. 4:23-24; 9:35-38; 21:14-16; Mark 6:4-6a; Luke 5:15; 6:17-19; 7:22-29; 8:1-2; 9:11.

10. Morna D. Hooker, *A Commentary on the Gospel According to St. Mark* (London: A&C Black, 1991), 72.

11. Receiving people after healing Peter's mother-in- law: Matt. 8:16-17. Jesus healed with compassion: Matt. 9:35-38; 14:13-14. Jesus was willing to heal: Matt. 8:2-4; Mark 1:40-45; Luke 5:12-14.

12. Hobert K. Farrell, "Heal, Healing" in *Baker Encyclopedia of the Bible*, gen. ed. Walter A. Elwell (Grand Rapids: Baker Book House, 1988), 1:938.

WEEK FOUR:

1. William Law, *The Works of Reverend William Law* (London: J. Richardson, 1762), 74.

2. Edward T. Welch, *Addictions: A Banquet in the Grave* (Phillipsburg, NJ: P&R Publishing House, 2001), xvi.

3. Akin, *Christ-Centered Exposition*, 192.

4. Ibid., 194.

5. Ibid., 196.

6. William L. Lane, *The New International Commentary on the New Testament: The Gospel of Mark,* 383.

7. Akin, *Christ-Centered Exposition*, 232.

8. The clear exceptions, other than the Shammai school of Pharisees, would have been the followers of John the Baptist and the Essenes.

9. David E. Garland, "A Biblical View of Divorce," *Review and Expositor* 84 (1987): 422.

10. Robert W. Wall, "Divorce," *The Anchor Bible Dictionary*, ed. David Noel Freedman (New York: Doubleday, 1992), 2:218; D. J. Atkinson, "Divorce," *Evangelical Dictionary of Theology*, ed. Walter A. Elwell (Grand Rapids: Baker Book House, 1984), 324.

11. Atkinson, 324; Note also that Josephus in *The Life Flavius Josephus*, 426-27, wrote that he "divorced (his) wife also, as not pleased with her behavior," and that he remarried. See Falvius Josephus, *The Works of Josephus: New Updated Edition*, trans. William Whiston (Peabody, MA: Hendrickson Publishers, 1987). Divorce, while not uncommon, was certainly not of the epidemic proportions of our day.

12. Klyne R. Snodgrass, "Divorce," *Mercer Dictionary of the Bible*, ed. Watson E. Mills (Macon, GA: Mercer University Press, 1991), 219.

WEEK FIVE:

1. Sinclair B. Ferguson, *Let's Study Mark* (Edinburgh: Banner of Truth, 1999), 181.

2. See Matthew 11:4-5; Mark 12:41-44; Luke 14:12-14.

3. *The Westminster Confession of Faith* (Atlanta, GA: The Committee for Christian Education and Publications, 1990), 8.

4. Three Dog Night, "One," in *Three Dog Night*, Dunhill Records, 1968.

5. Walter Kaiser, Peter Davids, F.F. Bruce, Manfred Brauch, eds., *Hard Sayings of the Bible* (Downers Grove, IL: InterVarsity Press, 1996), 442.

6. Edward W. Goodrick and John R. Kohlenberger III, eds., *Zondervan NIV Exhaustive Concordance* (Grand Rapids, MI: Zondervan Publishing House, 1999),1596

7. Charles Guignebert, *The Jewish world in the Time of Jesus*, trans. S.H. Hooke (New York: E.P. Dutton Company, 1951), 60-61.

8. James A. Brooks, *Mark*, vol. 23 in *The New American Commentary* (Nashville: Broadman Press, 1991), 185.

9. "Money Changer," *Baker Encyclopedia of the Bible*, vol. 2, ed. Walter J. Elwell (Grand Rapids: Baker Book House, 1988), 1484.

10. "Money Changers," *Holman Bible Dictionary* (Nashville: Holman Bible Publishers, 1991), 985.

11. John Lightfoot, Matthew—*Mark,* vol. 2 in *A Commentary on the New Testament from the Talmus and Hebraica: Matthew—I Corinthians* (Grand Rapids: Baker Book House, 1979), 432.

WEEK SIX:

1. John Piper, *Fifty Reasons Why Jesus Came to Die* (Wheaton, IL: Crossway Books, 2004), 119.

2. Tim Keller, *Jesus the King*, 192.

3. Ibid., 193.

4. Pierson Parker, "Crucifixion," *The Interpreter's Dictionary of the Bible*, 5 vols. (Nashville: Abingdon Press, 1962), 1:747.

5. Vassilios Tzaferis, "Remains of a Jewish Victim of Crucifixion Found in Jerusalem," *The Biblical Archaeology Review* 11 (Jan./Feb., 1985), 48.

6. Roy A. Stewart, "Judicial Procedure in New Testament Times," The Evangelical Quarterly 47, 1975), 95-109.

7. Ibid., 103.

8. Tzaferis, 48-49.

9. Ibid., 49.

10. Ibid.

LEADER HELPS

Thank you again for facilitating *The Gospel of Mark: The Jesus We're Aching For* with your group. If you read the introduction you found some tips for leading your group, but we wanted to provide more to make it as easy as possible for you.

If you are familiar with Bible studies that follow a daily homework plan, consider explaining to your group that they can read each week and break it up as needed or divide their time each day like this:

> Day 1: Read the Scripture passage from Mark that is listed at the top of each week.
>
> Day 2: Read Real Life and complete the activities in that section.
>
> Day 3: Read Real Truth and complete the activities in that section.
>
> Day 4: Read Real Ache and complete the activities in that section.
>
> Day 5: Read Real Hope and complete the activities in that section.

Encourage your group to complete as much as possible to get the most out of the study, but give grace knowing that the unexpected happens and sometimes we just can't do it all! Keep encouraging the women to come to the group time even when they don't have all the homework completed. It really is going to be OK!

There are some discussion questions on the Group Time pages to complete after the video teaching each week. Please feel free to create additional questions or use some of the ones here that will help them refer to their previous week of homework. This will help those who struggled with completing the homework stay connected with the group as they all discuss their answers or come up with their answers during the group time.

SESSION 1:

In addition to the questions on page 9, consider asking other questions that will help the group get to know one another at this first group time.

- *Who are the most important people in your life?*
- *How do you spend most of your time during the week? On weekends?*

SESSION 2:

Review some of the questions from Week 1 homework. Use these or others of your choosing.

- *What concern weighs most heavily on your mind today? (p. 13)*
- *Read 2 Peter 1:3-11. How would you synopsize this passage into one sentence? (p. 13)*
- *Someone once said, "Every saint has a past, and every sinner has a future." Do you think it's important to remember our past failures and if so, why? (p. 25)*
- *How has God's mercy steered you toward repentance lately? (p. 28)*

SESSION 3:

Review some of the questions from Week 2 homework. Use these or others of your choosing.

- *When have you been left stunned and/or giggling in the wake of a child's politically incorrect, but right-on-the-bullseye observation? (p. 36)*
- *What do you think Jesus meant when He spoke of the childlike requirement for entering the kingdom in Mark 10:13-15? (p. 36)*
- *What distractions most often prevent you from paying attention to what God is saying to you through both His Spirit and His Word? (p. 39)*
- *What would you describe as the common theme between Matthew 7:24-27 and Mark 4:1-20? (p. 42)*

SESSION 4:

Review some of the questions from Week 3 homework. Use these or others of your choosing.

- *Why do you suppose we find it so much easier to take offense and blame someone else rather than re-examine our own actions, attitudes, or beliefs? (p. 62)*
- *What teachings for your life do you see in Mark 6:7-13? (p. 64)*
- *In Mark 8:27-30, who did Peter declare Jesus to be? (p. 75)*
- *Who do you declare Jesus to be?*

SESSION 5:

Review some of the questions from Week 4 homework. Use these or others of your choosing.

- *How would you describe the drastic contrast between Jesus and His disciples in Mark 9:30-37? (p. 83)*
- *How does living on the historical "already happened" side of that very first Easter give us an advantage when it comes to understanding Christ's teachings? (p. 88)*

- *What real life situations tend to provoke your pride-disguised-as-insecurity to come out and play? (p. 91)*
- *How does James' ancient death (see Acts 12:1-2)—he was the first of the apostles to be martyred—compare to Christians who are being martyred across the modern world today? (p. 96)*
- *Which facet of Jesus-—the lion or the lamb —are you more comfortable leaning into? Explain your answer. (p. 101)*

SESSION 6:

Review some of the questions from Week 5 homework. Use these or others of your choosing.

- *What do you think God has taught you that you could have learned only through sorrow? (p. 109)*
- *How have you already seen the promise of Jeremiah 29:11-12 come true in your own story? (p. 111)*
- *Since the sacrificial system no longer exists, what modern day barriers have you observed—similar to the prohibitively high prices the money-lenders were charging for animals in Mark 11—that keep underprivileged people from worshiping? (p. 117)*
- *How would you describe the difference between an unhealthy "name it and claim it" doctrine and the type of faithful prayer posture Jesus advocates here in Mark 11? (p. 123)*

SESSION 7:

Review some of the questions from Week 6 homework. Use these or others of your choosing.

- *Do you have any close teammates who were formerly rivals? If so, how did the transition from foe to friend happen? (p. 138)*
- *If someone asked you, "Why did Jesus have to die?" how would you answer them? (p.142)*
- *When has there been a figurative veil-tearing moment in your spiritual life when you felt like a barrier between you and God was removed? (p.145)*
- *What's the "Oh wow, surely Jesus is the Son of God" moment in your life? (p. 146)*

LET'S BE FRIENDS!

BLOG

We're here to help you grow in your faith, develop as a leader, and find encouragement as you go.

lifewaywomen.com

SOCIAL

Find inspiration in the in-between moments of life.

@lifeKaywomen

NEWSLETTER

Be the first to hear about new studies, events, giveaways, and more by signing up.

lifeway.com/womensnews

APP

Download the Lifeway Women app for Bible study plans, online study groups, a prayer wall, and more!

 Google Play App Store

Lifeway women

BIBLE STUDIES FROM LISA HARPER

7 Sessions

Discover divine love in the often overlooked and misunderstood passages in Scripture, and find that Jehovah of the Old Testament is the same God we see through Jesus Christ in the New Testament.

lifeway.com/howmuchmore

7 Sessions

Discover some radically redemptive facets of pain and suffering while you learn how to engage with and authentically embrace the wounded world around you through the unlikely hope and joy that permeate even the hardest moments in Job's story.

lifeway.com/job

7 Sessions

Explore the action-packed Gospel of Mark—the first literary compilation of Jesus' earthly life and ministry—to lean further into His divine compassion in a way that might just change your life forever!

lifeway.com/gospelofmark

7 Sessions

Journey through the Book of Hebrews for an eye-opening and encouraging experience to help increase your intimacy with Jesus and deepen your faith in Him. He'll teach you not to falter when faced with personal difficulties or cultural persecution.

lifeway.com/hebrews

Lifeway women

Pricing and availability subject to change without notice.